Jewish Martyrs
Of Pawiak

JEWISH MARTYRS OF PAWIAK

by

JULIEN HIRSHAUT

HOLOCAUST LIBRARY
NEW YORK

Cover Design by Michael Meyerowitz
Printed in the U.S.A.
by Waldon Press, Inc., N.Y.C.

Julien Hirshaut, the Author

Contents

Part IV. Appendix

For my entire family, slaughtered by the Nazis, I light this candle in remembrance.

I also dedicate this book to the memory of my friends, the Jewish martyrs of Pawiak.

I Assume a Gentile Identity

Before the outbreak of World War II, I lived in Drohobycz, a town in East Galicia well-known for its oil wells and refineries. I got my law degree from the University of Lwow in 1933. Upon graduation, I was offered a position as legal advisor with the local branch of one of the largest banks in Poland. Shortly before the outbreak of war I was transferred to the main office in Warsaw.

Then came the war, and for the next three years I hid out from the Germans, living as best as I could. By the end of 1942 I managed to obtain a false birth certificate in the name of Michal Sawicki. Of my family, only my brother survived — he had set himself up in Warsaw with "Aryan" papers. I had made a mental note of his address, cherishing it in my mind as one would a precious gem for an emergency: No. 2 Ludna Street, in the neighborhood called Powisle (Vistula Riverside).

I arrived there with only the clothes on my back, and their condition was anything but elegant. Indeed, it was dangerous for me just to show myself in the street in such attire.

My brother lived with his wife in a room they had rented from a widow. There was enough space in their room for me. I actually spent a week there, but I agreed to shelter a stranger who had not registered with the authorities.

During that week I relaxed. From my brother's clothes my sister-in-law patched together a more respectable suit, one that would not arouse so much attention. Thus attired I was ready to go out into the "new world."

When my brother and I emerged into the streets of Warsaw one sunny summer afternoon, I looked about with a feeling of disbelief, like someone who had just returned from the hereafter. After all the traumatic experiences I had gone through in the past three years, the mild warmth of the sun shining out-of-doors and the normal movements of people in the streets were a revelation from heaven. I looked around me and, without changing the blank expression I had kept on my face, I said to my brother beside me, "I thought that the end of the world had already come, but here life goes on without a care."

My brother nodded in agreement and was silent again. He had just assumed the role of my guide and mentor. He had taken on himself the task of introducing me to a new and unfamiliar world, where peril lurked on all sides. "When one of our people first starts out here," he taught me, "he has to undergo a complete emotional transformation, down to his very guts."

I knew he was right; I had already undergone that transformation before I came. I had experienced it in an atmosphere of bloodletting. It was a pogrom, a liquidation of the ghetto, where kith and kin had been killed by Nazi murderers. At that time I lost all those near to me. I myself do not know how I survived the storm, and indeed why it was *I* who should have managed to survive.

A second important problem requiring a solution was that of identity papers, without which I could not register with the housing department as a legal resident of Warsaw. Luckily, my brother had a colleague, an attorney with whom he had practiced law in Drohobycz before the war. That colleague had certain "connections" who, for a price, could secure "genuine," i.e. not forged, identity cards. My brother gave his friend my birth certificate (false, of course), with the required photograph. The next day he received from him an official receipt with a number from the Municipal Authority of Warsaw. On that paper was written the date when I was to report to the City Hall to call for my identity card. Meanwhile, the receipt was considered as the official document.

The next step was finding a room for me. In the Polish newspaper published by the Nazis in Warsaw, my brother and I studied the classified sections. We noted the addresses of several interesting locations and set out to look at them. We limited ourselves to the neighborhood near the Three Crosses Square. We found a room we liked on Zurawia Street. The landlady was a middle-aged woman who lived alone in a five room apartment. Up to now she had rented only one room, to an elderly couple, refugees from Poznan. I would be the second boarder.

The room was located at the end of the corridor and separated from the others. I considered this an advantage, since its position would make it unnecessary to maintain contact with the other people in the apartment, and the less contacts, given my circumstances, the better. On the spot my brother paid a month's rent and it was agreed that I would move in the following morning.

Having solved the two most important problems, my brother and I returned home in an exalted frame of mind, but still I could not escape my depression. As we ate our skimpy dinner, he taught me how to talk so as not to betray my true origin. "The main thing," he explained, "is the look on your face and the expression of your eyes. They must show no sign of sadness or fear. Keep smiling and pretend nonchalance, no matter what happens."

*　*　*

There was another problem, a very important one: we had to eat. Somehow my brother had managed. For him, carrying the disguise did not create any great difficulty. The "mask" had become the natural expression on his face. For some years, at least since he had begun working in the legal profession, he had been living in an almost exclusively Gentile environment. Not only did he resemble a Pole in his external appearance but nothing in his behavior betrayed his Jewishness. He never lost his composure or his self-confidence. My brother had succeeded in making good friends among Warsaw merchants and had become a sales representative. Whenever legitimate business was slow, somehow he had found means of supplementing his income. He made friends with the smugglers who regularly crossed the Prussian border and brought back groceries to sell in Warsaw. The profits from this traffic could be substantial, but so were the risks. Before my arrival, my brother had gone on several such expeditions himself; I dissuaded him from continuing because of the great danger.

We agreed that I would eat dinner with him and his wife every evening and return to my room before curfew. But what was I to do with myself all day long? Remaining in my room all that time was impossible. My landlady must see me leave the house each morning, presumably for work. Staying with my sister-in-law was all right on occasion; but making a daily routine of it would have aroused the suspicion of my brother's landlady and the others who lived in the same building.

Caught up as we were in a world of cruelty, these "trivia" became major factors determining life and death. My brother sought by all available means to eliminate obstacles and anticipate dangers. "Tomorrow," he said, "we will visit a businessman I know with whom you can work." The wholesaler in question dealt with personal and household cleaning products. The spacious storage facilities which this businessman owned on Marszalkowska Street contained a row of bins displaying a variety of floor waxes, cartons of shoe polish and various soaps which, because of the war situation, were in short supply.

My brother introduced me to the businessman as a friend of his who had come from the countryside looking to earn a little money. "My friend will visit the hardware stores in town," he said to the businessman. "He'll take orders and then buy from you whatever his customers want."

The wholesale businessman, an elegantly-dressed, prosperous-looking individual, eyed me with a friendly smile. He seemed pleased that we had come. He gave me a current price list of his goods and remarked that they were presently in great demand on the market. I studied the list for a few minutes and left him on a genial note. I went out into the street an accomplished businessman!

Before we parted, my brother warned me to keep looking about me to see whether anyone was following me. If I saw anything suspicious, I was to get away as fast as possible. He named several neighborhoods to which he said I must never even come near. I wandered about the city. Warsaw now seemed quite strange, for I had not been there in some years. I found myself in an area where, apparently, there were offices set up by the German occupation authorities. There was a sentry post in front of each building and the street was empty of passersby. The guards looked at me with their steely gaze and I, apprehensively, began to look for ways to get out from that neighborhood, unnoticed. My fear left me only when I was lucky enough to reach a busy street filled with civilian traffic.

Slowly, I got accustomed to my new occupation. Every morning I went out and visited several businesses, taking whatever small orders the owners gave me. Then I went to my wholesaler, got the merchandise and made the deliveries to my customers. My earnings weren't very big, but they covered my modest daily expenses. The entire routine of dealing with a few stores and my wholesaler, took no more than two or three hours. When I was finished it was still too early to return to my room on Zurawia Street or to go to my brother. I would walk about the streets and, if I passed a church, I'd go inside and pretend to pray. In that way I got through another hour of the day. As time went on I became better acquainted with the neighborhoods through which I wandered. I added a few churches to my circuit, so I could visit a different church every day and not appear too often in one place.

When I returned to my room in the evening, I wanted nothing more than to relax on my cot, wipe the "mask" from my face and immerse myself in thoughts which I then could not reveal to anyone. But one evening, after I barely had a chance to stretch my weary legs, there was a faint knock at my door. It was the landlady, Mrs. Sobolewska, asking whether I wouldn't like to come in to her dining room for a glass of tea. I couldn't refuse, so I went.

Mrs. Sobolewska was of the impoverished nobility. She had celebrated her fortieth birthday not too long before, but she looked a lot older. She was thin and walked slightly stooped. Her complexion was dark and patches of grey had begun to appear in her black hair.

When I entered the dining room, Mrs. Sobolewska was sitting at a table, and opposite her sat another woman, a fleshy blonde with blue eyes. She appeared younger than Mrs. Sobolewska, but she may have been older.

The landlady introduced us. The blonde was a friend of hers, who was living nearby. They had got lost in conversation and hadn't noticed that it was past the curfew hour, the landlady explained, and so her friend would have to stay at her place for the night.

Naturally, the conversation at the table turned to the events of the day, particularly the situation on the battlefronts. Hitler was doing badly. The Russians were in hot pursuit. The Italians were being beaten. How long would the house painter be able to last?

"That's all very well," Mrs. Sobolewska said, "but what finally happened to that German whom they shot in the street today?"

I thought the question had been put indirectly to me. The people in the apartment building believed that I was "someone from the organization," from the underground, taking orders from the Polish Government-in-Exile, who were fighting against the German occupation. I had never told anyone directly that I had any connection with the organization, but I had dropped some hints from which they might surmise that I was "one of them." I hoped that if people believed I was in the underground, my life would be more secure.

I tried to answer my landlady's question in the manner of an underground activist. "Yes," I said, "that Nazi was a war criminal. He murdered our heroic fighters. So our agents read to him the death sentence from the Underground Tribunal and then carried it out on the spot." Mrs. Sobolewska seemed to enjoy my answer very much. She then asked other questions for which I always had a convincing, patriotic answer. But at one point she said something as follows: "Certainly none of us approves of what Hitler is doing; we don't care for the Nazi way of handling the Jews. Still and all, we owe him some thanks for doing our dirty work for us." I was shocked but had prepared an answer for such an eventuality: "Neither the Polish Government-in-Exile in London, nor its Delegate's Office in Warsaw, will ever approve Nazi crimes. Neither will they approve the consequences of such crimes."

But I never got to give my little speech. The plump blonde, who up to this point had sat in silence, suddenly knocked a full glass of boiling hot tea from the table. The glass shattered with a crash, and the blonde moaned that she had burned her foot. At that moment I glanced at her and saw in her eyes a provocative glint. I felt a sudden stab of fear in my heart. Who was this woman? I got up from my chair. I stood motionless for a moment, while Mrs. Sobolewska hurried to help her friend. While the two women knelt on the floor picking up pieces of glass, I hastily bade them good night and returned to my room.

* * *

One afternoon when I came to my brother, I found him sitting gloomily at the table. He told me that his friend, the lawyer who had provided us with our identity cards, had been arrested. It seemed that agents of the Criminal Police had been following him for some time. They had wanted to nab him with his wife, but she had managed to get away.

"Are we going to have trouble with our papers?" I asked anxiously. My brother too was tormented by the same thought. But then he began to examine the problem by applying some common sense and arrived at the following conclusion: If the arrest of his friend had any link with those who had provided the "Aryan" identity papers, the Criminal Police would have had his address from the very beginning; the agents could have arrested the couple at the same time without any difficulty; they would not have had to follow the husband. Rather, reasoned my brother, his friend had been betrayed. But, we can breathe easily, he concluded, because this affair has no connection with our papers. At that moment it seemed to me that my brother's reasoning was altogether sound. But I never found out whether he was really right. A few hours later I myself fell into the hands of the murderers; I never saw my brother or my sister-in-law again.

This is what happened. The next morning I went out as usual and headed for Marszalkowska Street where my wholesaler had his business. He packed up a few bundles of merchandise. I paid him a larger sum of money than usual. I told him to hold on to the change, that as soon as I had delivered these goods to my customers, I'd be back for more.

I went outside again and got on a streetcar. I got off at the street where the stores of most of my customers were located. After I had walked only a few steps, I felt that someone was following me. When I turned around, I saw I was surrounded by several Polish underworld characters. One, a blond with a pockmarked face, looked at me with a pair of droopy eyes; he looked as though he were ready to go to sleep.

"What do you want?" I asked in a firm, nonchalant voice.

"Don't play dumb, Jew!" he barked.

Meanwhile, the group around us had grown. Opposite me I saw many faces, some smiling, some laughing out loud.

"Look! They caught a Jew!" Everybody seemed really happy.

I no longer had the bundles of merchandise; they grabbed them from my hands. Forcing myself through the crowd I began to walk away rapidly. I barely reached the end of the street when out of nowhere appeared a German policeman. He pointed his rifle at me and ordered, "Halt!"

At the police station I was searched by a higher-ranking German officer. He found a gold wedding ring sewn into my vest; he pocketed it without embarrassment. After he was through with me, he sent me directly to Gestapo headquarters on Szuch Avenue. That interrogation, conducted by Brand himself, lasted somewhat longer. I made believe I did not understand any German, that I was a simple peasant with no idea of what they might want of me.

After a routine examination, Brand concluded that I was not circumcised and, therefore, not a Jew. Pending further investigations, however, he decided to send me to Pawiak the following morning. A guard brought me to a cell downstairs. There the chairs were lined up in the same manner as the seats in a streetcar. That was why the Gestapo jail on Szuch Avenue was popularly known as the "streetcar." The guard pointed to a chair where I was to sit, admonishing me not to talk, not to move, not even to turn my head. So people sat there like mummies.

By that time night had fallen. But I could not even think of sleep. Lonely thoughts crowded my brain, penetrated the soul and shook my spirit. It wasn't a feeling of self-pity, pity for a life which seemed inevitably about to end. Quite the contrary. I accepted my probable death as a relief — the end of a nightmare through which I had lived up to that moment. Reminders of recent experiences in the ghetto passed through my head. There was my little girl, whom the Germans had killed on the very threshold of her life. She had been playing so happily, on the day they took her away; what had she done to deserve death?

My wife: she had disappeared at the very height of the "action." Where was she now? Was she still alive and perhaps looking for me?

My elderly mother: she had been terribly sick, but they had dragged her out of bed and made her walk. And when she could not walk, they shot her on the spot. And the other members of our large family: my sister, her husband, their two children, and my brothers, their wives and their little ones. All of them surfaced and paraded before my eyes as though they were still alive.

Was it worthwhile fighting just to keep alive when all of them were already dead? A whole world, past and future, had been annihilated root and branch. What value would my life have after all that?

The next morning, as I rode through the streets of Warsaw in a covered Gestapo van with a group of other prisoners, I looked through a crack in the tarpaulin cover and saw traffic moving in the streets as if nothing had happened. I felt no desire to become a part of such a normal life; I had made peace with my fate. So I was deep in thought when the van rolled into the prison yard. I arrived at the administrative offices in a state of bewilderment. From there I was brought to Block Eight, which occupied half of the huge prison basement.

Brand had not believed that I was a Jew. But every newcomer to Pawiak underwent a physical examination by a doctor. The doctor was a Pole and a prisoner himself. With a wink at the prison guard, he said, "This one is circumcised."

The guard walked over to me and asked, "Are you a Jew?"

"No," I replied.

But the guard was not listening. He rewarded me with a resounding slap and a kick with his studded boots. "Why don't you admit it, you dog?" he shouted. "Are you trying to deceive the German police?" Bleeding profusely, I was flung into a cell. The heavy door slammed shut. I looked about me through

21

clouded, dazed eyes. Several dozen Jews were standing about — the inhabitants of cell 258. I was actually happy that I could be together with Jews again, that I would no longer have to wear the mask on my face.

* * *

My situation during the year I spent in Pawiak was most peculiar. Three weeks after my arrival, I was brought back to Szuch Avenue for further questioning. This time I was seen by the Gestapo officer in charge of Polish prisoner-affairs. After I had answered a few questions, he informed me of my sentence; together with other Polish inmates, I was to be sent to a labor camp in Germany. The verdict sounded too good to be true: I knew that after the report of the Polish doctor in Pawiak I would never be able to leave the prison as a Pole. In Pawiak I was considered a Jew and put in the death cell; on Szuch Avenue I was treated as a Pole.

Only much later did I find out why the Gestapo never discovered my true identity. Leon Wanat, head clerk of the main prison office and a prisoner himself, had assumed the task of destroying any damaging evidence in the files of the prisoners. No doubt the doctor's report never reached Gestapo headquarters. Wanat was probably instrumental in saving my life, and the life of many other prisoners. For this he deserves special tribute.

Part I

A PRISON
CALLED PAWIAK

Chapter 1

The Island of Death

The prison was called Pawiak, a name familiar to all who lived in Warsaw. It was a huge prison, which the Czarist rulers had built in the nineteenth century when Warsaw had been part of the Russian Empire. In Czarist times it was the main prison of central Poland where political prisoners and criminals alike were incarcerated. Why it was erected in the northern section of Warsaw, the very heart of the Jewish quarter from time immemorial, remains a mystery.

Pawiak occupied a vast site stretching along the entire length of Więzienna Street. The front of the structure faced Dzielna Street; the back looked out upon Pawia. Hence the name "Pawiak." Ironically, the drab street had a name that meant in Polish "The Peacock Street." The massive main building had three floors; it measured over two hundred meters in length and seventy-five in width. It stood almost in the center of a big yard, surrounded by high, thick walls. Built like a fortress, pockmarked with tiny barred windows, it was well-suited for its purpose — to isolate the unfortunates who were confined within its walls from the rest of the world. Only the central section facing the front had large, normal-sized windows. The administrative offices were located on the ground floor. On the second floor of this section there were two large halls, formerly used for cultural events. The Germans attached these two halls to

Block Four and converted them into prison cells for Jewish artisans. On the third floor there was a Catholic chapel and a small synagogue for the prisoners. Since the Nazis were not particularly devout, the chapel now stood empty. When things got especially "hot," when the Gestapo was rounding up huge transports to be sent to the concentration camps, the chapel was used as a room for hasty interrogations. The holy paintings which adorned the walls of the chapel were witness to hideous scenes of beating and torture, laments and groans.

The huge yard surrounding the prison was further secured on all four corners by watchtowers manned day and night. In the yard were also several smaller structures, housing supply rooms, workshops, infirmary, kitchen, bathhouse, and boiler room.

LAYOUT OF PAWIAK BUILDINGS

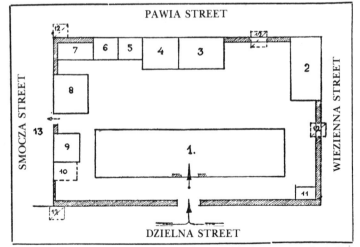

1. Main building; 2. Factory building (from which the ten Jews, including the author, later escaped); 3. Boiler room; 4. Bathhouse; 5. Big kitchen (for the prisoners); 6. Hospital; 7. Small kitchen (for the guards); 8. Large supply rooms; 9. Small supply rooms; 10. The scale, which also served as the gallows; 11. Garage, where the belongings of the dead were sorted; 12. Watchtowers; 13. Entrance to women's prison; Walls around the prison yard.

Desolation

By the time I arrived in Pawiak on July 8, 1943 the entire Warsaw ghetto was a wasteland. There was rubble everywhere, jagged walls were all that remained of the large and handsome dwellings now charred and blackened by smoke. Gaping at me through wide, burned-out windows were the inside walls of these buildings, some of them still adorned with wallpaper or paintings. They told me of a former life of hard-working, peace-loving people. Here and there light pierced through large holes in the painted walls. The gloomy, hopeless reality of the present seemed to be mocking the past it had ravaged. The Pawiak loomed like an island of death amidst a sea of ruins and desolation.

A Brief History

One of the prisoners in my cell was Chaim Finkelstein, a man in his late fifties who had once been an antiquarian in Warsaw. He was no newcomer to Pawiak. In the days of the Czar he had been imprisoned on charges of revolutionary activity. He frequently recalled how the Russians had treated the inmates of Pawiak. We envied those earlier prisoners for, although the Czarist regime was by no means a liberal one, and although the cultural level of the Russians was — according to Goebbels' demonic propaganda — inferior to that of the Germans, life in Pawiak under the Czars was a bed of roses compared with what we endured under the Nazis.

It was in Czarist times that the well-known escape of the "Ten from Pawiak" took place: ten Poles imprisoned for national revolutionary activities were freed by the Underground. Although we had heard details of this legendary escape many times, Finkelstein never tired of repeating the story: members of the Polish Revolutionary Organization seized a carriage and rode into the prison yard disguised as Russian gendarmes. Telling the official in charge a trumped-up tale, they got the prisoners out. True, it sounded like a fairy tale even to us but we knew from history that it really had happened, and we admired and envied those ten fortunate Poles.

Under Nazi Rule

Before the last war, Pawiak was a prison for criminals; one block was reserved for political suspects who were detained only for the investigation. After the Nazi occupation of Warsaw, Pawiak became the main prison for all Poles suspected of political subversion. It was soon crowded with Poles arrested on various charges, or for no reason at all. The prison had a maximum capacity of fifteen hundred, but under the Nazis there were never less than three thousand inmates.

For the Polish prisoners Pawiak was only a transit station. Following investigation and a brief period of internment, the Gestapo handed down its verdict. The rules by which the Gestapo conducted its trials were a mystery. The prisoner had no right to defense; his sentence was not even read to him. Once his trial was over, one of four things might happen to him: If he was very lucky, or his family was able to bail him out, he was set free. Many of the younger prisoners were sent to the punitive labor camps where they worked for months before being sent to Germany for forced labor. Those less fortunate, about eighty percent of the prisoners, were sent to the concentration camps. Each week a transport of several hundred inmates was sent to Auschwitz or to Grossrosen. A purge took place every three months — the entire prison was emptied out and additional thousands were sent to the concentration camps, making room for new victims. Within a week or two at the most,

Pawiak was again jammed with prisoners. Executions of Poles took place constantly but the tempo was stepped up in the last half of 1943. By the end of the German occupation, thousands of Poles had met their death on the gallows.

Permanent Residents

As a rule, Polish prisoners did not remain in Pawiak for longer than three months. Most of them were eager to leave. Here they were under constant threat of death, suffering under a prison regime that was cruel and relentless. Some Poles, however, managed to settle down more or less comfortably and adapt to prison life. They worked in various functions, made friends, and were on good terms with the guards. Because most of their families lived in Warsaw, they made every effort to remain in Pawiak as long as possible and to avoid deportation to the camps. A small number of these Polish inmates stayed in Pawiak for many years. Among them were three Polish doctors who worked in the prison hospital. They served time from 1940 until the summer of 1944 and were set free by the Germans just before they evacuated the prison.

The Polish clerk named Leon Wanat who kept the prison records was also a "permanent" inmate, having been in Pawiak since the first day of the German occupation. The Germans did not let him out because he knew too many of their secrets. Well aware of this, Wanat took advantage of the first available opportunity to make his escape; he regained his freedom shortly before the Warsaw uprising.

The small group of Polish artisans — most of them tailors and shoemakers — employed in the Pawiak workshops were also permanent residents. They were not deported because the Germans needed their skills. About one hundred fifty Jewish artisans were also permanent inmates. They would never be set free, nor would they be deported. The only road open to them was the road to death. As long as the Germans needed their labor, they were kept in Pawiak, given their daily rations of watery gruel, and forced to work until the last ounce of their strength. They enjoyed a "special" privilege — the right to work or to be promptly executed. Nor did the transports include the handful of true criminals serving out sentences imposed on them by the Polish authorities before the war. These felons were looked upon as "aristocracy" by the Germans.

Jewish Prisoners

Up until the destruction of the Warsaw ghetto in April 1943 only Jews seized on the "Aryan" side were confined in Pawiak; those arrested in the ghetto itself were kept in the "Gesia Street" prison (so-called "Gesiowka").

When a Jew from the "Aryan" side was locked up in Pawiak, he remained there until the next "Action" (mass deportation from the ghetto). During the "Action" he was sent to the *Umschlagplatz* (assembly point for deportation); from there he started on the last journey to the extermination camp in Treblinka.

When I was brought to Pawiak, there were no longer any Jews in the Warsaw Ghetto. The Jewish prisoners were taken directly from Pawiak to the execution site, located on the ruins of a buliding on 25 Dzielna Street, directly opposite the prison gate. The site was moved subsequently to Zamenhof 19, in the courtyard of the former *Judenrat*; (this location served for execution of Poles as well).

Selected from the most vicious criminals Nazi gendarmes performed their grim task dressed in white uniforms. We called them the White Gendarmes.

Whenever we looked out of our barred windows

and saw these fiends, a shudder would run through us. Their ugly, swollen jaws jutted out from beneath their helmets. The younger ones had ascetic faces with thin, cruel lips. Their eyes were spiteful and merciless. The White Gendarmes exterminated tens of thousands of human lives: old and young, men, women, and children.

The Jews of the "Befehlsstelle" (Command Post)

After the execution, the White Gendarmes would leave the area; the Jews of the *Befehlsstelle* then disposed of the dead. These Jews represented a particularly painful episode in the history of Warsaw's destruction. The group consisted of several dozen youths and girls, most of them from the lowest strata of the Warsaw Jewish underworld. Their leader was Trisk, a corpulent Jewish coachman from Powisle.

While Jews were still living in the ghetto, these young people had applied to the Germans for jobs. The Germans installed them in the building of the Gestapo *Befehlsstelle* on Zelazna Street, facing the ghetto, and assigned them the task of clearing the ghetto of the dead.

Whenever there was an execution in the ghetto itself, the *Befehlsstelle* Jews accompanied by a guard of the White Gendarmes would drive up in their little wagons, drawn by small horses. They would load the dead onto the carts, bring them to the yard of Zamenhof 19, and burn them. Frequent executions of Poles also took place in the streets of Warsaw. In such cases the Germans themselves transported the dead, via auto, to the stakes. A primitive auto-da-fe was set up on the execution site. The *Befehlsstelle* Jews tossed the corpses onto a pile of dry wood, covered them with a second layer of wood, poured on gasoline and set fire to it.

After the Warsaw Ghetto Uprising, the Germans

were determined to liquidate the ghetto. The *Befehlsstelle* Jews were most helpful in revealing the hiding places and bunkers, even dragging out the few remaining Jews. The handful of survivors from the Warsaw ghetto will always feel loathing and contempt for these despicable traitors of their own brethren.

In the end, even the members of the *Befehlsstelle* did not go unpunished by the Nazis. Early in 1944 the Nazis accused them of plotting an uprising. Allegedly, several members of the group were found to be carrying weapons. The Gestapo locked up the *Befehlsstelle* Jews in Pawiak and kept them in isolation for several days. One morning, as I walked through the prison yard, accompanied by a Ukrainian guard, I saw a huge pile of corpses in a corner under the wall. The Ukrainian told me that those were the "Jew Boys" (*zhidy*) of the *Befehlsstelle*, adding with a confidential wink, "They finished them off last night."

Thus ended the chapter of the *Befehlsstelle* Jews. Even they did not escape death.

The next day we saw a new group busying themselves with the dead. They were Jews from the Lodz ghetto.

The End of Pawiak

Pawiak eventually met its demise. When the Nazis burned down Warsaw, after suppressing the Warsaw Uprising, they also bombed Pawiak.

When I returned to the spot after the liberation in 1945, I stood gazing at the devastation — "Is that all that is left of this infamous place?" How insignificant and fleeting is man's arrogance and criminal conceit. Pawiak, the unvanquished symbol of German power, lies here before me, demolished and crushed. And I, the helpless human, who was destined to be its victim, am here as a witness to its destruction.

As I stood there overcome with emotion, I had a

vision of things past. I saw rows and rows of the thousands of my comrades who met their fate in this hell on earth.

I saw their frightened hollow eyes, I saw the agony on their faces when they were led on the last road to death.

I saw old men praying "Shema Israel" (Hear O Israel) — going to their death without fear, with God's name on their lips. I saw young men and women cut down in the prime of their life.

I saw little children paralyzed with fear, too numb to cry.

I came to my senses, turned around, and fled. But I could still hear the lamenting and sobbing of the martyrs. The ringing in my ears bore a distinct message: remember and tell, remember and tell . . . .

Never again do I wish to lay eyes on this abomination, but I must revive, once more, the horrendous events of that era.

Chapter 2

The Last Jewish Community in Warsaw

Jewish Workers in Pawiak

With a fury unmatched in the annals of history, the Nazi assassins completed the bloody destruction of the Warsaw Ghetto. During the Warsaw Ghetto Uprising and after the liquidation of the ghetto, the German police, abetted by the SS, burned down every last vestige of Judaism. The persecution of Warsaw Jews bore a special character, unlike the persecution of Jews in other Polish cities. In addition to implementing Hitler's program of total extermination, the minor German officials took revenge on Warsaw Jews for daring to carry out the uprising, for daring to oppose them — the uncrowned rulers of the world. The extermination of Warsaw Jewry was total and merciless. In other Polish ghettos the Germans allowed small groups of Jews to remain at their jobs after liquidation; in Warsaw every Jew they could find was slaughtered.

Several months before the destruction of the Warsaw Ghetto, the Gestapo formed a Jewish labor group in Pawiak. A group of about a hundred to a hundred and fifty Jewish artisans — mostly tailors and shoemakers — were employed in the prison's workshops. They were housed in the prison, and every Sunday they were given permission to go into the ghetto to visit those of their families who were still alive.

After the Uprising, the artisans were confined to their cells. One morning, early in May 1943, a special squad of gendarmes arrived in Pawiak, with orders from the Extermination Commandant for their execution. The artisans were led out into the yard and forced to undress. In their underwear, they were loaded into automobiles and taken on their last trip to the ghetto. Shivering and in cold sweat, the Jewish artisans were brought to Zamenhof 19 where they were gunned down.

Only seven artisans, those with the most useful skills, were saved by the Gestapo prison guards, who hid them when the gendarmes came for them. The seven became the nucleus of Pawiak's second group of Jewish artisans. The Germans soon discovered that they could not get along without the Jewish workers. Not only were they master craftsmen, but as Jews, they could be treated as slaves without rights. Grateful as they must be for the opportunity of living a little longer, such slaves could be exploited, made to work hard and at top speed, tormented and preyed upon to one's heart's content.

In the meantime, the Nazis' "glorious" battle in the Warsaw Ghetto was over. The liquidation was complete. Only the small number of Jews who had settled on the "Aryan" side before the Warsaw Ghetto Uprising had survived, but their lives were far from secure. Most of them had to remain in constant hiding. A few (those who didn't look like Jews) could walk about the streets of Warsaw. For both groups, nonetheless, the danger of being recognized by Germans or Poles was ever present.

In addition, Warsaw was a magnet for Jews from every corner of Poland. It was the biggest city in the land, the easiest place in which to "disappear." Every day Jews from the provinces descended upon Warsaw. They surmounted thousands of dangers to get to this city. Here they hoped to find refuge and live free from persecution and fear. It is estimated that there were twenty thousand Jews on the "Aryan" side of Warsaw at that time. Arczynski, treasurer of the "Zegota" (Council for Aid to Jews), believed the total to be fifty thousand, but the estimated figure of twenty thousand provided by the Jewish members of the Council seems more accurate.

These Jews were engaged in an unending, tense struggle to stay alive. The Gestapo used all its resources to discover and annihilate the survivors. But with superhuman strength and endurance, these human shadows pitted themselves against the giant machine of the enemy. Driven from place to place, forced to find new documents, assume new disguises, the persecuted played a game of cat and mouse with the persecutors. Too often, alas, the Jews on the "Aryan" side fell into enemy hands and landed in Pawiak, thus bringing to an end the days of wandering.

The Germans had ample numbers from which to choose craftsmen for their depleted work force. Each month an average of five hundred Jews were brought to Pawiak. The nucleus of seven craftsmen was soon joined by fellow recruits.

This second group never totalled more than one hundred and fifty Jews. It was no easy matter for a Jew locked up in Pawiak to attain the indescribable good fortune of being admitted to this labor force. Some of them were employed in the prison workshops. Others were forced to toil at more difficult tasks such as digging sewers.

There was also a group of Jewish auto mechanics who worked in the Gestapo garages on the site of the former sport stadium at Dynasy Street. At first, these mechanics were attached to the Polish labor force on Gesia Street. In December 1943, this group was transferred to Pawiak and combined with the Jewish work force.

Life was intolerable for the members of the Jewish labor force. During the day they had to work very hard; at night they were locked up in their prison cells and devoured by vermin. There was never enough to eat, and those who couldn't manage to obtain food by their own ingenuity, simply collapsed. In addition, there were the constant persecutions by the German prison guards and their Ukrainian helpers.

Although the life of these Jews was so tormented, their spirits embittered and their future dim, they bore on their frail shoulders the responsibility for upholding the honor of the last of Warsaw's Jewish community. They lived their hopeless lives conscious of their sacred mission: it was up to them to carry on the tradition of the glorious Jewish *kehillah* to preserve its memory, to be its symbolic future.

Chapter 3

Death Chambers

Jewish Prisoners and the "Plus-Jews"

Cell 258 was located in Block Eight of the Pawiak cellar. Although only Jews were confined there, it was not the actual death chamber. The Jews in cell 258 were the Jewish prisoners taken into custody on the "Aryan" side on suspicion of being Jewish. During interrogation by the Gestapo, they never confessed to this "terrible crime." On the contrary, they argued, they were the most devout and purest of Christians, natives of this or that locality with relatives still living there. The answers had to correspond with the data appearing on the false documents confiscated by the Gestapo. A prisoner who tried to outwit his cross examiner by stating that his relatives were already dead had to furnish proof of their former address; he even had to know in which cemetery they were buried. The Gestapo interrogator jotted down every word of the prisoner's statements. He then proceeded to conduct an investigation. In the meantime the suspect sat in cell 258 as a prisoner (*Häftling*). The average investigation took about six weeks. But if the accused claimed to have been born in a distant and remote place, it might take the Gestapo as long as three months to complete its investigation — three months in which the suspect could hope to live!

Interrogation of the male prisoner was a lost case even before it had begun. No matter how well he conducted himself, a circumcised Jew was endowed with the "corpus delicti" from which he could not rid himself. (Only Jews were circumcised in Poland.) With Jewish women it was different, especially when they could present "good" identification papers. I knew of a number of cases where the investigation proved favorable and the women were set free.

So the arrested man sat in cell 258 and waited for a miracle. Time passed, and the investigation was over. The prosecutor had evidence that the prisoner was lying, and this was sufficient proof of his Jewishness. The case was closed, the Gestapo was through playing games, and another Jewish name was promptly added to the list of the next deportation (*Umsiedlung*). In other words — the death sentence.

The Gestapo then forwarded this list to Pawiak's administrative office. The Jew's name was removed from the list of "prisoners" and marked with the "plus" (+) sign, meaning that he no longer belonged to the world of the living. The prison guard removed him from cell 258 and took him next door to cell 257 — the death chamber. Now the man knew without any doubt that tomorrow he would be a corpse.

The doomed man was not alone in cell 257. Every day several Jews sat there waiting. They were the ones caught on the "Aryan" side, and because of their Jewishness — a pre-established fact as far as the Gestapo was concerned — thrown into Pawiak with a clear-cut sentence of *Umsiedlung*. They would sit in cell 257 only until their execution the next morning.

In the same way as an orderly housekeeper tidies his home every day, collects and throws out the rubbish, so the prison guards disposed of the "Jewish rubbish" every morning. The prison was run with typical German efficiency and punctuality. The "plus" Jews were led out to the execution site; the death cell was empty, though never for more than a few hours. Punctually at twelve noon, the automobiles would drive in, crammed with fresh victims from Szuch Avenue, the lovely tree-lined street on which Gestapo headquarters were located. Once again, cell 257 was filled with "plus" Jews.

In Cell 258 — A Mixed Bag

There was a strange mixture of people during my stay in cell 258. Of the twenty-eight prisoners, twenty-three were Jews; the other five were the usual Gypsies or idlers with no profession. These five prisoners caused the rest of us a great deal of trouble.

The twenty-three Jews came from a cross section of various backgrounds. Among them were several longstanding Warsaw residents, with names well-known to Jews and non-Jews alike, a substantial number of intellectuals, doctors, lawyers and engineers. Some of them had been converted to Christianity before the war, others merely possessed false certificates of baptism. All hoped to be spared by the Germans. They had been accepted by Polish society, had lived for decades among Gentiles without anyone suspecting that they were Jews. But once unmasked by the Hitler gang the convert was treated like any other Jew.

Some of my fellow inmates in cell 258 came from the Warsaw underworld. There were also two eighteen-year-old boys in the group.

The first time I entered cell 258 I was in a state of confusion. I stood for a moment in the middle of the cell, looking around me. The first thing I noticed was the Jewish faces of the inmates; immediately I felt more comfortable, as though I had returned home after a long journey. "Are there so many Jews anywhere else in the world?" I wondered.

I was ashamed of this foolish thought. Actually there were no more than a handful of Jews as unfortunate as I was. What was there to be surprised about?

A man with marked Jewish features and naked to the waist was sitting on the floor in the middle of the room. Beside him was a tin wash basin. His hands were immersed in the dirty, rust-colored water from which protruded the soaking ends of a rag; he was washing his shirt. When I was hurled into the room so unexpectedly, this man paused and stared at me. I stared back. There was a gentle smile in his eyes, and a flicker of human feeling. Such a display of emotion — no matter how slight — was new to me, because for a long time my life had been an ordeal. Hounded by enemies everywhere, driven from place to place by savage beasts, who constantly threatened my existence, I had almost forgotten that there were still human beings in the world.

Those gentle eyes drew me. I took a step toward this Jew, eager to engage him in conversation. "Why are you washing that shirt?" I asked him. "What difference will it make? They'll kill you regardless of whether your shirt is clean or dirty."

"I've been here three weeks," he answered quietly, almost apologetically. "I don't know how long I'll have to stay. In the meantime, I don't want to be eaten up by vermin."

The other prisoners surrounded me, asking questions about what was going on in the world, especially about what was happening on the war fronts and how far away was the Red Army. These were vital problems still of interest to the half-dead prisoners. Their only hope of freedom lay in the immediate defeat of the Nazis. They had no need to read the newspapers. Through the eyes of their exhausted souls, they could predict events. A week before, a new prisoner had told them that the Soviets had occupied Tula and were approaching Oriol. Italy was on the verge of capitulating to the Allied forces. Could this be the end of the war? Was it possible that during the past week events were beginning to move in this direction?

If the war didn't end today, or tomorrow at the latest, the inmates of cell 258 would not live to see the end of it. How long did these prisoners have to live? A day or perhaps a week, and the miracle must occur during that time. If not? The Jewish prisoner in cell 258 did not think about that. He knew the answer. It was the unspoken word — death.

So I told my new cellmates all the news I could, hoping to encourage and cheer them up. The reports from the fronts were hopeful, I thought. But my new friends were disappointed. In their fantasy, events had moved much more rapidly, and here it turned out that the Russians were still very far away, and the Allies were progressing too slowly. What could they hope for now?

They sat in silence on their straw mats, each deep in thought about his bitter fate.

At Work

Gradually I grew accustomed to my surroundings. I became friendly with the Jew who had been washing his shirt when I first arrived. He was from Lublin, and his name was Fishman. Although he looked like the Jew he was, he had lived in Warsaw with his wife and child on "Aryan" papers. Since he had no money, he had had to find a job. He found work in a German office, but his Polish co-workers soon realized that he was a Jew; within a short time the Gestapo seized him. He knew that his life was over. He hoped his wife and child would be able to escape from the Nazis, although without funds this would not be an easy matter. Fishman's anxieties had made him sick. One ear was giving him trouble; he was in great pain and could hardly hear. But Jews in Pawiak did not get medical treatment.

42

Now it was quiet in our cell. Exhausted from heat and hunger, we sat on our straw mats. Nobody felt like starting a conversation. Since it was almost dinner time, we waited eagerly for the little bit of watery soup that would be doled out. Suddenly the heavy door was flung open. The Kapo, a young Gentile with savage eyes, stood on the door sill brandishing his long leather whip, shouting, "Jew-boys! To work!"

We jumped up. The Kapo looked around as though searching for someone and asked, "Where is your *Starosta*?" (The *Starosta* was the elected leader of the prisoners in his cell.)

Kazik, a fine man from Bialystok, stepped forward. "Here I am, sir."

"Eight Jews must go to work right away. Select them yourself. If you won't, I will, and that will be worse for you, Jew-boys!"

"Immediately, Mr. Kapo. Right away . . . you'll get your eight workers," Kazik assured him.

There was an unwritten law in prison that the Jews of cell 258 were assigned the hardest and dirtiest tasks. We were always prepared to be called to work at any moment. In order to avoid beatings, we had arranged ourselves on a priority list which we pledged to follow whenever the call came. The old and the weak were exempt from labor.

Each one of us knew when it was his turn; thus when the Kapo needed eight workers, these men promptly left the cell. Since I was a recent arrival, I was one of the eight. We went out into the corridor, where we were met by a Ukrainian guard who led us out into the prison yard. We walked alongside the wall until we reached the appointed spot.

Burning coals and ashes lay in huge piles in the yard. They were glowing with black, choking smoke rising from the heaps. The coals had just been wheeled out in iron carts from the large boilers which provided steam and hot water for the kitchens, the bathhouse and the other prison buildings.

We were commanded to shovel the glowing coals into the iron carts and drag them to a pit at the other end of the yard, then fill the pit to the top, level with the ground. For us starving and exhausted Jews this task was almost unendurable, particularly as the coals gave off a truly hellish heat. Painful burns resulted from handling the pieces of hot coals, or from accidentally stepping on one of them. The smoke burned our eyes; the tears streamed down our cheeks; we could not breathe; our lungs felt as though they would burst; our bodies were covered with searing wounds. But we did not dare to stop working even for one moment. Several Ukrainian guards and one German SS man kept watch over us. Kolenko, the Ukrainian, was the most vicious of them all. I met up with him again at a later period when I was assigned to work in the bathhouse. In that capacity, I was "entitled" to somewhat more lenient treatment and even Kolenko was very friendly and affable, especially when he needed a favor from me.

Now, however, when Kolenko stood over us, he resembled a ferocious beast. I was the first one in the group to collapse. I just stood there unable to raise a finger. Kolenko ran over to me. Seizing my iron shovel he beat me on the shoulders and arms with it. If that were to happen today, I would not be able to withstand such an assault. But in those days, we seemed to be made of iron. I felt dizzy and there were red sparks in front of my eyes. My whole body ached; I couldn't lift my arms, but I managed to remain on my feet. I was lucky — if I had fallen down, I would have been shot. The life of a helpless Jew, one no longer capable of productive work, had no value in Pawiak.

I continued to work, my legs shaking and my hands

trembling. Whenever I had a shovel full of coals and tried to carry it over to the cart, the coals scattered all over the ground. On my right stood Herman, a big man of forty odd years with a beefy face and Polish mustache. Herman could hide his Jewish identity. He even told us, his closest friends, that he was a Gentile, a pure Pole. His family supposedly came from Kolomyja (Galicia) where, he assured us, there were many Poles named Herman. Somehow, we sensed that Herman was not telling the truth. Since the Gestapo had locked him up with Jews, they probably had a "good" reason. We had no time, however, to dwell on Herman's problems. We all had our own troubles. Herman was entitled to his little game of make believe. Maybe it would save his life.

Herman stood on my right, hauling the heavy, loaded shovel with his last ounce of strength. Kolenko watched him for a little while, then walked over to him. Herman groaned and moved his hands mechanically as fast as he could. The shovel began to slip out of his grasp. The coals flew to the ground and fiery embers bit into his legs and mine because I was standing only several steps away.

Kolenko was already standing beside Herman. Just as he had done with me, he seized the shovel from his hands. Herman was sure that now he too would get a beating and instinctively bent to one side. But Kolenko only said in a hoarse voice: "You fat Jew! Watch me and you'll learn how to load a shovel!"

With rapid movements Kolenko began to pile the coals onto the wagon. He worked quickly. This was no wonder because he had the strength for it — he was not starving, like us, nor was he exhausted. Kolenko gave the shovel back to Herman. "That's the way to work. If you don't, I'll shoot you on the spot."

This time Herman had been lucky.

In the meantime I had begun to feel a little better. I

was still in pain, but I was calmer. My hands had stopped shaking and my legs no longer gave way. Not far from me stood Michalek, one of our two youngest prisoners. He was about eighteen years old, an emaciated boy with a pale face. Still almost a child, Michalek had already experienced more than many an adult. He came from a good family in Warsaw. His father, Dr. Kahan, was an eminent surgeon who had fled to Russia. Michalek was certain that his father was still alive.

Michalek himself had endured much. Nevertheless, he was carefree and witty, with a joke for every occasion, every situation. He laughed at everyone and managed to handle any kind of job they gave him to do. Now he filled up and emptied his shovel very deftly; he was the first to load up his cart. Then he began to toss coals into my cart, laughing and whispering in my ear. "One of these days we'll finish 'em off. That boor and imbecile," he nodded toward Kolenko, "was born for this kind of work. He knows the shoveling business well. Must have been doing it all his life."

Kolenko walked over toward Michalek. "Why are you gabbing so much?"

"I said, Mr. Prison Guard, that the pit is full already and there's no room for any more coal. If we dump these wagon loads into the pit, it'll be filled over the top."

"Take care, you dog! I've got an eye on you!" Kolenko yelled in German and threatened him with the whip. Nevertheless, he realized that the job was finished. He told us to drag the loaded wagons to the pit and leave them there; then he took us back to our cell.

It was long after dinner time when we returned to our cell. Our eight bowls of soup were already standing in a corner on the stone floor. Kazik, the *Starosta* who distributed the soup, had set them aside for us. Like starving animals we flung ourselves on the food. That day, the soup happened to be thicker than usual — it contained more beans. It had grown cold and we had no spoons, but it didn't matter. Like dogs, we squatted and pushed our mouths into the bowls; like dogs, we slurped it down. In no time our bowls were empty, but our hunger was far from appeased. There was nothing we could do except wait for the evening soup. In the meantime, we tried to get some rest. But now the wounds on our legs began to burn intensely. My right arm was almost paralyzed from the beating it had received.

Kettles of Hot Soup

Our bellies are our timekeepers. Young Michalek is the most accurate at telling the time of day. When twelve o'clock approaches, he can be heard saying in his deep, masculine voice which jarred with his childlike face and figure, "We'll be getting dinner soon."

Michalek is never wrong. No sooner does he utter these magic words, than we hear the clanging of the huge tin kettles. The orderlies are bringing them into the kitchen to fill up with the soup for our dinner. A quarter of an hour later we hear more noise in the corridor. The orderlies are returning with the heavy, hot kettles.

The Kapo unlocks one cell at a time. The prisoners step outside carrying their bowls. An orderly pours a ladle of soup into each bowl. The prisoners go back into the cell and the Kapo locks the door behind them. Then he unlocks the next cell and once more the soup is poured into the bowls. The German prison guard stands there all the while, keeping an eye on the entire procedure, making sure that all is in order.

The Prison Guards

Every section has two German prison guards, and each German guard has a Ukrainian helper. These two prison guards alternate duty every day.

We know our two prison guards only too well — and no wonder! We call one of them the Rat. We don't know his real name and no one really cares. What *is* important is that he is a sadist of the most vicious sort. He looks like a rat — short, hump-backed and skinny with a yellow face, his small eyes glaring with hatred.

Recently he ordered Czaryski, a lame young man from Lodz, out of the cell. We had no idea what "crime" Czaryski had committed, but the Rat ordered him to stretch out on a bench and then proceeded to beat him mercilessly with a long, leather whip. Another prisoner, a Pole whom the Rat had ordered to assist him in this exercise later told us that the Rat had had an orgasm during the beating session.

The Rat is most brutal towards Jews. He is prepared, at a moment's notice, to shoot all the Jews in his charge — every single one. He will do it with great love when the command comes. Since the command has not yet been issued, he avenges himself on the Jews in every way he can. He tells the Kapo to withhold the tiny bit of marmalade they usually get for breakfast; he instructs the orderlies to pour off the water from the soup and give only that to the Jews instead of the soup itself. A devout believer in Hitler's racial doctrine, the Rat is diligent and zealous in implementing Hitler's program for the annihilation of the Jews.

The other German prison guard in our block is Alpman; he is more kindhearted than the Rat. He speaks fluent Yiddish and Polish. A Volksdeutsch from Lodz who was brought up among Jews, Alpman

From right to left: The prison guard of the Jewish section Knädelseger; the executioner Kurt Nowotny and the guard of the eighth division Alpman.

insists on speaking to them only in Yiddish. Two categories of Jews enrage Alpman: those who truly know no Yiddish and those who disclaim knowledge of the language in an attempt to hide their Jewishness.

Once he even came passionately to the defense of the Yiddish language. One of our cellmates was Frank, a Polish major of Jewish descent. Alpman asked him a question in Yiddish; Frank did not understand him — he really did not know Yiddish. Alpman refused to believe that, flew into a rage and attacked Frank. Throwing him to the ground he began to kick him, all the time shouting in Yiddish, "How dare you to deny your mother tongue?"

Normally, Alpman was not cruel. He treated us no worse than he did the Gentiles. Whenever he was on duty, we received the same treatment the Polish prisoners did. He never beat us and often he showed us some compassion.

Finagling

The most popular word in Pawiak was *finagling*. The word covered a multitude of activities, from *finagling* a second bowl of soup to *finagling* a job in the Seventh where the Kapo was a decent Pole who gave the Jewish workers plenty to eat.

The knack for *finagling* played a major role in our everyday routine. Very often the unfortunate prisoner could make life a little easier for himself. There were no lack of *finaglers* in cell 258. When it was the Rat's tour of duty, Czaryski would station himself in the doorway of the cell half an hour before dinner time, bowl in hand. Czaryski believed that the first spoonful of soup was the thickest, and was worth the long wait.

Finally, the Kapo flings open the door and shouts: "Everybody out for soup!"

Czaryski with the lame leg is the first on line near the kettle. He gets the first spoonful, and we all wish him well — may he enjoy it.

Opposite him stands Salek Tenenbaum, whose talent for finagling is even greater than Czaryski's. He never tries to be the first one at the soup-kettle; he is out for greater profits. Salek was a waiter who had worked for years in a small restaurant on Wola Street. He had connections with the underworld and was an experienced gambler. Short and dark, he describes himself as a clever man, a man with brains. When we are called on to do a job of work, he can tell at a glance whether the work will be difficult — will we be beaten — or easy — with the possibility of getting a piece of bread, or something even better.

When Salek has sniffed around and determined that the job is a good one, he is always the first to apply. It does not bother him that it may not be his turn. No one stops him anyway; we're in no hurry to go to work; who knows what surprises are in store for us. But Salek almost always comes back with something to eat. Recently, he brought an entire loaf of bread and a tin of fat. He sat all by himself in a corner and ate so much that he got sick to his stomach. He didn't get off the pot all night. We, his cellmates, were miserable. The air in our cell was foul to begin with, and now, with the pot standing uncovered all night, the stench became overwhelming.

One time I was sent on a job together with Salek. We were called to work by Alberts, a Gestapo official from the prison's administration office. Alberts led us into the garage, used for storing the clothing and shoes of those who had been executed. Salek was experienced in this kind of work, and I was supposed to be his assistant. Without a word, Alberts took us into the garage, locked us in, and left.

Salek proceeded to instruct me: "Take every piece

out of the sack, examine it thoroughly to make sure there is nothing hidden inside. Whatever you find in the pockets must be thrown onto a heap; then you make separate heaps for the garments: one for trousers, one for shirts, jackets, etc."

I was stunned. It was the first time I had come into contact with the personal belongings of the slain victims. "These are the clothes of dead Jews," I thought. Inside these sacks standing about on the concrete floor of the vast garage, I envisaged living people, anguished souls all lamenting their dreadful fate.

"What are you dreaming about?" Salek called out. "You should be happy. This is a good job. It's easy and you can always find something in the pockets. You'll find lots of bread. Come on, get going."

Robotlike, I went to work. I wasn't thinking about bread at all. At that moment I would have been incapable of chewing; the bread would have stuck in my throat. In one of the jacket pockets I found an American twenty-dollar bill. Salek saw it and stretched out his hand.

"Hand it over."

"What are you going to do with it?" I asked.

"We have to give it to Alberts."

"What are you talking about? Do you want to make that murderer richer than he already is? He's got plenty!"

"Well, what do you think we should do?"

"Tear it up." I told him. "Tear it into shreds right now."

"And if they find the torn pieces?" asked Salek fearfully.

But I wasn't listening. I ripped the bill into shreds and, with a sense of relief, tossed them into a corner under a pile of rags.

The last sack to be sorted out was small and only half full. I put my hand inside and pulled out a dress

51

— the little green dress belonging to a five- or six-year-old girl. My heart almost stopped beating. In my memory I saw a horrendous sight: Germans and Ukrainian police are leading a mass of people — mostly women and children. The women are screaming and the children are crying. The police are beating them with big sticks, striking them on their heads, shoulders, wherever they can. Among the condemned group is a little girl, my little daughter, wearing a dress almost identical to the one I now held in my hand.

"What are you doing? Don't just stand there." Salek roused me from my trance. "He'll be back any minute, we've got to finish."

"I can't go on," I said. I couldn't get the horrible scene out of my mind. "Please, Salek, finish the job yourself."

Salek must have scrutinized me carefully; when he returned to the cell, he told the other prisoners of my behavior. I was pale as a corpse, he said and he had been afraid I would collapse. "Such weakness," he said, "does not become a man. You must never give in."

The others listened to Salek, and were silent. When he finished his story, nobody said a word. Even the two boys, Michalek and Mardex, who were constantly bickering, slunk into a corner and were quiet. The cell had become as quiet as a graveyard.

"Here's your bread," said Salek, giving me the crusts he had found in the pockets of the dead.

"I don't want any," I told him. "You take it."

Faster . . . Faster . . .

It is after six o'clock in the evening. From our window we can never see the sun. But a single golden sunbeam, tinged blood red, has found its way into our dark hole. It creeps along the corner between the two walls opposite the window; then wanders slowly upward along the wall from the floor to the ceiling, growing gradually smaller until it dissolves in the darkness of our cellar twilight.

There is a sudden commotion in the corridor. Heavy doors are opened; there is shouting in Polish and German. "Faster! Faster!"

The sound of rapid footsteps intermingles with the voices, the footsteps of many people running as though someone were pursuing them. The voices fade into the distance, it is quiet; two minutes later we hear the same footsteps, the same people running back. The wild outcry: "Faster! Faster!" pursues them; they run into a cell, with the clanging of heavy chains, its heavy door slams shut.

Now our cell door is flung open and the Kapo yells. "Toilet!"

We know only too well what this word means. We are being let out to go to the toilet. We are prepared to make the dash. Two of us, whose turn it is today, will drag the heavy bucket filled with excrement. The others run with their basins in their hands.

"Faster! Faster!" the command rings in our ears.

We race like the wind through the long corridor, and our two comrades, carrying the full bucket try to keep pace with us. They are having difficulty, but they dare not lag behind; if they do, they will be thrashed by the prison guard. Now we have reached the toilet and we run inside. On the way — still on the run — we have unbuttoned our pants. There are two regular toilet bowls plus several pails and ordinary pots. All these receptacles together can accommodate no more than ten people. The rest of us wait for those who are seated to get up, so we can take our turn.

The toilet attendant is a Polish prisoner selected by the prison guard. His is a nasty job. The attendant must clean the toilet — the "throne" — and pour out the contents of the ten pots and buckets. But the prisoner assigned this revolting task considers himself fortunate: he has become a "functionary." No longer confined to a closed cell, he can stay in the open service quarters where life is more comfortable and the food more plentiful. The toilet attendant enjoys unlimited power over the prisoners during the time they spend in his "turf." Whenever we get there, he is there waiting for us with his whip and his eternal yell:

"Faster! Faster!"

The entire "toilet time" allotted our group must never exceed two minutes. During this time we must empty and rinse out the big bucket, and fill our individual basins with clean water tor washing ourselves. Since no more than ten people can use the toilet at one sitting, each of us has about half a minute to relieve himself. The toilet attendant keeps a sharp eye out to make sure we observe the rules. Sometimes one of us is sick and needs to sit longer. But the attendant won't allow it.

"Faster! Faster!" he shouts to the man on the pot. He continues this refrain while beating the culprit with his whip until the poor fellow jumps up and runs off.

The toilet was a nightmare, a race against an onslaught of savage screaming. Each of us had another dream which we were sure would never be fulfilled — in our fantasy we were allowed to sit on a toilet as long as we wanted, ten minutes if necessary.

We Are "Häftlinge" (Prisoners)

We have returned from the toilet. Once more we are in our cells behind locked doors. We stand pressed close together in small groups. Exhausted from running, we gasp for breath. Some of us have been whipped. Old Yuzhviak (we didn't know his real Jewish name) had been struck on the head with a whip. A long, red streak zig-zagged down his face starting from over his right eye and going to the other side of his forehead. The wound had festered and was now turning blue.

Yuzhviak is about seventy years old. He has thick grey-white hair. He doesn't look like a Jew. For many years he had been the manager of a large insurance company. Although he was half-assimilated, he still considers himself a Jew, his suffering has merely strengthened his faith in God. Twice a day he prays in the prison cell. He prays surreptitiously and silently but we cannot help noticing the rapid movements of his lips and the ecstasy in his eyes.

Yuzhviak can not believe that Germans are capable of murdering Jews and innocent people who have harmed no one. He is convinced that the Jews whom the Germans have deported are working somewhere, and that after the war they will all return home alive and well. Yuzhviak's illusions stem from his profound faith, his belief in the power of the Almighty in this world.

God would never allow a weak and innocent human being, especially a child, to be unjustly hurt, Yuzhviak maintained.

Now he stands in the middle of the cell, his eyes bloodshot, staring into space with an uncanny expression. He presses a wet cloth to his head, groaning softly. The wound is very painful, but I suspect he is suffering more from his shattered faith.

It was a Pole who struck him, not a German or a Ukrainian. What is more this Pole was a toilet attendant, like Yuzhviak a mere prisoner. By all the rules of logic and justice, this Pole should be a friend, not an enemy.

For the first time, Yuzhviak finds himself doubting his beliefs. The foundation of his faith has been strongly shaken. If a comrade, a fellow prisoner, has dared to give him, old Yuzhviak, such a cruel beating just because he was unable to get up from the toilet at the exact moment — what reason then is there to complain about the Germans, our overt enemies?

Yuzhviak presses the wet cloth to his head, groans and broods. In the meantime Herman, the so-called "Aryan," is running around the cell in great agitation. He is oblivious to the fact that he keeps bumping into groups of his cellmates. The groups break apart under the impact of his huge frame. Herman is bewailing Yuzhviak's calamity: "Jesus Maria!" he shouts. "What kind of people are they? Are they Poles! To beat up a comrade, a compatriot! That's unheard of! A shame and a disgrace on us Poles! On the entire nation!"

Suddenly the sound of a bell is heard in the corridor, and a deep, masculine voice calls. "Get ready for roll call!"

We don't waste a minute because we know that today is the Rat's tour of guard duty. We form three rows, with *Starosta* Kazik at the head of the first row. We are ready. We don't have long to wait. The door opens and the Kapo enters. The Rat stands at the doorsteps of the cell. He won't go inside because he is afraid that close contact with the "dirty Jews" will contaminate him. But he can't refrain from a malicious remark. "How are you Jew-boys getting along in your cage?" And he laughs savagely.

We don't answer, but Kazik the *Starosta* announces in broken German, "Herr Wachmeister (prison guard), I respectfully report that the twenty-eight prisoners of cell 258 are present and accounted for."

"What did you say?" screeched the Rat. "Not prisoners, just Jews! Do you understand, you dog? You are Jews? Start over again, once more, from the beginning!"

This issue has been a bone of contention for a long

time. In reality we *WERE* prisoners, and we were reluctant to forfeit our rights as prisoners, whatever they were. The same argument ensued at almost every roll call over which the Rat "presided." Kazik would report "prisoners" and the Rat would correct him: "No! It's Jews and Gypsies." When the Rat was in a hurry, or happened to be in a better frame of mind, he merely corrected Kazik and left. At other times, he didn't say word.

But today, the Rat was in a viler mood than usual. We noticed it as soon as he appeared in the doorway and prepared ourselves for a clash. He commanded Kazik to repeat his announcement; Kazik did not open his mouth.

The Rat became hysterical. "What?" he screamed, drawing closer to Kazik.

Kazik stood erect, motionless, as though he had heard nothing.

"Will you report?" the Rat yelled into his face.

"The prisoners are here," Kazik repeated calmly.

The sound of a sharp slap rang out, and then another. Kazik, his face fiery, remained standing, erect and motionless. The Rat reached for his whip, for some reason he did not have it with him. Furious, he ran out of the cell. The Kapo slammed the door after him. The Rat did not return that evening. At subsequent roll calls, Kazik continued to report "prisoners," and the Rat did not react. He must have become reconciled to the idea that Jews merited the distinction of being classified as "prisoners," even in the eyes of the Germans.

The roll call brought an end to our day in prison. Then, engulfed by silence and the stillness of a dark night in Pawiak, each of us was left alone with his thoughts. During these dark and sleepless nights, as the prisoner lay open-eyed on his hard, stinking straw mat, he would relive his entire unbearable ordeal.

During these black nights some of us, in our imaginations, hatched fantastic schemes of rebellion. A tiny spark of hope might be fanned into a flame of courage and heroic deeds. Many were those who were immobilized by despair, a prisoner's worst enemy. Despair could lead to the grave. During those dark nights, something whispered to me that I *WOULD* survive this place. But when I thought about it rationally, it seemed no more than a pipe dream. No doubt many of my fellow inmates spun this same fantasy of survival and freedom; unfortunately, only two from cell 258 were lucky enough to remain alive.

Several years after the war, I heard from Kazik, the *Starosta*. He was a survivor and had settled in Israel.

Chapter 4

Slave Labor

Jewish Workers in the Gestapo Garages

One Sunday afternoon in the middle of August 1943 several Gestapo men entered our cell. They caused a great commotion, screaming and beating up some of the prisoners. Then they ordered us to go out into the corridor and line up.

We exchanged glances: "This is the end." How could it be anything else? Our last hour had struck, and we were being taken out to be executed.

The Gestapo men called on each of us in turn to step out of line and asked, "What is your trade?"

What should we answer? We knew that tailors and shoemakers were being assigned to the group of Jewish artisans in Block Four. So we figured that mentioning either of these two vocations might not only save our lives, but would make us eligible for transfer to that lucky group. Each of us chose a different trade. Michalek said he was a bootmaker; Mardex, a tailor; Wdowinski, a young engineer, said he was a locksmith. The older prisoners were not adept in the art of lying: Segalovitch, a seventy-year-old engineer from Warsaw, formerly a representative of the *Zeisswerke* told the truth.

All the prisoners who had reported were told to stand against the opposite wall. I was one of that large group. Still, the Gestapo did not seem satisfied. Apparently, they had not found what they were looking for.

Now came Herman's turn to report. He tried another tack. "I'm an auto mechanic."

"Is that so?" said one of the Gestapo men. "What kind of work do you specialize in?"

"I was a foreman in a garage."

"Stand against the other wall."

Finally we realized that they were looking for auto mechanics. In any event, those chosen were better off working on a job than rotting in a death cell. Five more so-called auto mechanics promptly joined Herman.

Kazik, the *Starosta*, standing next to me, was part of the larger group of rejectees. He looked around him, blinking his shrewd eyes. He was waiting for an opportune moment when he saw the Gestapo men talking among themselves, not paying attention to us, Kazik made a dash for Herman's group of six. I imitated him. Our ploy worked. The Gestapo counted us and now we were eight. We were led away; the others remained behind.

A Gestapo guard took us to the former ghetto prison on Gesia Street. Alpman, the prison guard who conducted us as far as the gate, told us: "Jews, you can thank your God that you're leaving this place. No matter where you go now, you'll be better off."

Still, life was not much easier on Gesia Street. In those days it was the site of a punitive labor camp for Poles; it also housed fifty Jews, the remnant of the former huge Jewish labor camp of the "Ostbahn" (eastern railroad).

The Ostbahn was liquidated in June 1943 but the lives of this small group was spared. The Nazis put them to work on Dynasy Street. We were assigned to this group of fifty.

I shared the good fortune of the garage workers

for only about ten days. We were dressed in dark green camp uniforms. I was given a pair of short pants which barely reached to my knees. The jacket was too short and so tight that I couldn't move my arms. We were awakened each morning at four A.M. Then we stood for two hours in the yard during roll call. The mornings were cold that August of 1943. Moreover, we were inadequately dressed, undernourished and suffered from lack of sleep. Roll call, which our tormentors used as an occasion for more beatings, was dreadful.

We walked to work, about four kilometers each way and always in the gutter. This march, closely guarded by a large group of SS, exhausted us both physically and morally. We dragged ourselves through the streets of Warsaw from Bielanska to the Theater Place, Krolewska and the Krakowskie Przedmiescie to Dynasy Street. Everything we saw, the splendid and vital city, basking in the rays of the warm sun, the green trees, the lawns and flower-filled squares, the handsomely dressed, smiling populace seemed dreamlike, signs of an unattainable alien world. What were we but mere shadows of former human beings. We belonged to a world already dead which had lost every contact with life. We had lost our families, our health, our possessions; and now, looking like ghosts with half-naked bodies and exposed legs peering from tattered inadequate clothes, we formed a grotesque procession. Not one of the passersby spared us a glance. This daily march to work was a most painful, demeaning and humiliating experience for us.

Our work was hard, the food even more meager than in Pawiak. The nights on our stinking cots were sleepless — millions of bed bugs attacked us the moment the lights were put out. I used every ounce of my failing strength not to give in. There was an opportunity to escape; several Jews who had maintained contact with the "Aryan" side, Kazik among them, took advantage of it. I still had a brother hiding out in Warsaw on "Aryan" papers, and I planned to make my escape and stay with him. But because of one careless mistake, I lost this chance for freedom. Lange, the Gestapo foreman of the workshops, stopped me almost at the last moment. I was locked up in the "dark" cell on Gesia Street for twenty-four hours. From there, I was brought back to Pawiak.

Hanging was the punishment for an attempted escape. All the way back to Pawiak, I had one vision: by the next day my corpse would be dangling from the gallows in the prison yard, a grim reminder to the inmates of Pawiak of what awaited them. I still don't know by what miracle I escaped death. After several days in the death cell, I was transferred to Block Four which housed the group of Jewish artisans.

In the Fourth Block

It was the dream of every prisoner in cell 258 to be transferred to Block Four — I was one of the lucky ones. The life of the prisoners in Block Four was just as uncertain as anywhere else, but in Block Four you could look forward to a vegetative existence for at least as long as your services were useful to the Germans. Besides, living conditions in Block Four were not as harsh. Workers got all the bread they could eat, the sleeping quarters were more comfortable, and there was, to a certain extent, more freedom to move about. If life in 258 was a process of dying, in Block Four it went up a notch to become a process of vegetating.

I was assigned to the bathhouse for disinfection duty. I tended the huge, black steam cauldron in which all the clothes were "sterilized." When a group of prisoners came to bathe, I led them into a special room, told them to take their clothes off and tie them into a bundle. While they were in the showers, I put the bundles into the cauldron, closed the lid and released the steam. The clothes would stay in the steam about three quarters of an hour. Then another prisoner opened the cauldron from the other end, removed the hot clothes and returned them to their owners. It was no secret to us that the disinfection process did the lice no harm at all. The little creatures emerged from the steam bath as hale and hearty as before; not so our clothes. Made of inferior goods, our wartime clothes came out in shreds.

The Six Bath Attendants

Five more Jews, in addition to myself, worked in the bathhouse. We had very little in common and sometimes found it difficult to adapt to each other. Our ages varied greatly, we came from different backgrounds, different cities. Still, we made a great effort to find a common language and gradually we did succeed. We accepted our situation and tried to make things as comfortable for ourselves as possible under the circumstances. We spent all day until late at night in the bathhouse. There we ate, breathed easier and sometimes even had a chance to relax. In the evening, after work, we returned to our cells and to the other Jews in our group. I am convinced that even under these harsh conditions we might have developed an interesting and creative life had it not been for the ever present threat of death.

As bathmaster, the Ukrainian prison guards held unlimited power over the workers, as well as over the bathers. The guards were rotated frequently during the time in which we worked there. Some guards were humane and easy to get along with; others were vicious men who enjoyed terrorizing the prisoners. But generally, we were on good terms with our prison guard. We even managed to "tame" one of them, Kowalenko, a man notorious for his cruelty. Kowalenko lived in peace with us, and because we had "tamed" him, he no longer posed a threat to the bathers. The only really vicious one in the lot was Kostenko. No matter how we tried, we couldn't pacify him; fortunately, he only stayed a short time.

The Underground Mail

The six Jewish bath attendants also fulfilled an invaluable political and social function which helped thousands of prisoners, most of them Poles.

In ancient Rome the city baths were the central meeting place of the Roman patricians. A comparison between the aristocratic residents of the Eternal City and the several thousand tormented prisoners of Pawiak only *seems* ludicrous. The Pawiak bathhouse was the only place where prisoners had an opportunity to make contact with each other. Every inmate had to visit the bathhouse at least once a week. Every cell block was assigned a different day and was escorted there by prison guards. To prevent contact between the prisoners of different cells, each cell was taken separately. Only after one group had finished bathing was the next one brought in.

Obviously, communication between the various cells and blocks was of vital importance to us. The bath attendants took upon themselves the role of go-between. We initiated an ingenious "postal system." Naturally, we had to maneuver in strictest secrecy to avoid discovery by the Germans. It was a risky business because the greatest "crime" a prisoner could be accused of was possession of a forbidden, uncensored letter, known as a gryps.* Nevertheless, our enterprise functioned efficiently and unerringly.

The bathhouse routine made our task possible. The

* *Gryps* — a letter smuggled out of prison.

prison guard of a particular block brought his charges to the bath, counted them and gave the list to our Ukrainian guard. We were on good terms with most of the Ukrainians; they never spied on us. While one of us would engage a guard in conversation, the rest of us were able to go ahead with whatever had to be done. First, we gave each prisoner the *gryps* which we had previously set aside for him. Then we distributed pencil and paper to those who had to write an answer, or who wanted to send out their own *gryps*. We hid these letters in a secure place, distributing them to the addressees when their turn next came.

This postal system broke through the prisoners' isolation, an isolation on which the Gestapo depended for its investigative procedure. It was the prisoners' only chance to communicate with each other on matters of importance.

For example: The Germans had taken two Poles into custody on trumped-up criminal charges. To ensure that they would not give identical replies at the interrogation one was sent to Block Three, the other to Block Five. The Germans had planned this procedure with their usual thoroughness. They knew that if the two prisoners lied, their replies would contradict each other; such contradictions were just what the Gestapo wanted. Thanks to our system, the prisoners were able to come to a mutual agreement regarding their testimony. The replies they gave at the interrogation were almost always identical. The Gestapo was frustrated and enraged, but could never discover the reason for the identical answers. Indeed, our ingenious mail system was never discovered.

In Pawiak there were always a certain number of prisoners kept in solitary confinement. They were the leaders of the Polish Underground, high-ranking officers of the A.K. (Armia Krajowa, Polish Home Army) plus pilots and parachutists of the Red Army and the R.A.F. taken captive on Polish soil. These people were classified as major criminals, charged with instigating and abetting the Polish resistance movement, at that time, a thorn in the flesh of the Germans. These men sat in single isolation cells in Block One, guarded by the Gestapo night and day; even the Ukrainian guards had no access to them.

At one time, there were five celebrated "solitaries" in Pawiak: an R.A.F. officer named Kennedy; three Polish colonels, Strusiewicz, Karanski and Rostworowski; and Jerzy, a Polish parachutist from London. When the Germans brought these five to the bathhouse only we the attendants were allowed to remain. The Gestapo guard stood close by to make sure they didn't talk to each other or to us.

Finding a way to communicate with them was a knotty problem: a single careless move could have resulted in death, but we were not afraid. Our lives were forfeit anyway and could be extinguished for the merest trifle — a cigarette, a too-slow movement, a facial grimace. We ignored the additional danger. Under the very eyes of the Gestapo, we established contact with the solitaries.

The brief moments they spent in our company were of the utmost importance to these isolated prisoners. How else could they hope to establish contact with the Polish Underground? We knew the underground was making an all-out effort to liberate the five. A rather curious incident occurred involving the prison guard Lysenko, a man notorious for his cruelty and harassment of the prisoners. We had heard that the Poles were now executing great numbers of Germans and traitors, so we added a request of our own; we sent a message to the underground asking them to "finish off" Lysenko. A week later we received an amazing reply: "Your 'boy' must not be harmed. Remember!"

At first we did not understand the message. But

when we thought about it, the matter became clear. Lysenko was in Pawiak performing a double role — he was actually working for the Polish Underground. Although he could take messages in and out of the prison, he was unable to communicate directly with the five solitaries. He had to rely on us as intermediaries.

How did we solve the various communication problems? There were two systems: the first and most important was the disinfection cauldron. When the solitaries came into the bathhouse, they gave me all their clothing for disinfection. I would remove the *gryps* meant for the Organization and hand them over to Lysenko. There were other letters, too, with various questions and requests for cigarettes, matches and writing paper. We filled these requests as best as we could. Our replies, plus the *gryps* which Lysenko had given us, were placed in their clothing and returned to them after the disinfection process was completed.

Another way of communicating with the solitaries was by pre-arranged secret code. The only person who could possibly decipher this encoded language was Chaim Finkelstein. He manned the water apparatus and in this capacity stood close to the prisoners while they were showering.

Finkelstein was a man over fifty, bald and almost totally blind, with huge spectacles on his long nose. At first glance, he looked like a simpleton. All day he stood beside his water apparatus, turning the two valves — the larger one for cold water and the smaller for hot — trying to keep the temperature at a constant 40° C. Finkelstein was a shlemiel — the temperature kept jumping from 20° to a sudden 60°, forcing the bathers to dash out of the shower. There was a thermometer on the water apparatus but Finkelstein, with his bad eyes, could not make it out.

The bathers, knowing Finkelstein's eye problem,

would shout, "Mr. Finkelstein, it's freezing in here!"

Finkelstein would adjust the smaller valve and the bathers would cry out in unison, "Now it's perfect, very good!"

These innocent remarks from the regular prisoners were a part of the code.

Finkelstein's system worked just as well for the solitaries. For example, he would say very calmly, "Sir, if the water gets too hot, let me know right away!"

To the Gestapo man standing near Finkelstein, the remark held no significance. But for Strusiewicz, it contained the answer to a question he had posed a week ago in a letter written to us. And he would mutter, irritably, "The water is too hot, Finkelstein."

The Gestapo man suspected nothing, but Finkelstein understood the "complaint." Kozakiewicz, Kapo of Block Three and a link in the underground, was to pick up the *gryps* which now lay hidden among the disinfected clothes.

This was how we six tormented Jews fought the powerful Gestapo machine. Did we win? I don't know. One thing, however, is certain: we undertook the struggle, and to a great extent we did achieve what we had set out to do.

Self-Help

We also instituted a secret self-help program through which Jewish prisoners who suffered from hunger and lack of cigarettes were helped by some of the Polish prisoners working in various food-related departments of the prison administration. (Jews were not allowed to work in such services.) These compassionate Poles brought us supplies to distribute among the needy. Since we were the only source of communication between the prisoners, we automatically became the center of distribution for the underground self-help movement. Sacks of bread, other supplies and cigarettes were stored with us which we in turn distributed to the bathers.

Who were the needy ones? The thousands of Polish prisoners confined to their cells — ninety percent of the prison population. Only ten percent of the inmates were functionaries.

We also wanted to help the Jews incarcerated in the concentration camp on Gesia Street. "Concentration Camp Warsaw" was established in October 1943. It has taken into custody over five thousand Greek, Slovakian, French and Hungarian Jews; they were then sent to work clearing away the rubble of the former ghetto. Their living conditions were appalling; these people were slowly starving to death, and we did everything in our power to help them. We were assisted in this task by other Jews in our group. In January 1944, the Germans transferred our group from Block Four to the new building. Before the war it had been the residence of the prison guards; now it housed the workshops. The Germans integrated it to the prison, built workshops on the first and second floors, and reconstructed the third floor into prison cells for the Jewish craftsmen.

This building stood outside the high wall surrounding the prison; the windows of our cells looked out on Wiezienna Street at the edge of Pawia Street [the German guard was less strict in that area]. We had an unobstructed view of the devastated area. By now a large part of the ghetto had been cleaned up and leveled. In this vast sea of emptiness one structure remained standing, visible to us from afar, the concentration camp on Gesia Street. Formerly a prison, it was surrounded by numerous small barracks built by the Germans to house the thousands of prisoners brought there from almost every corner of Europe.

Those Jewish inmates had at one time been dignified, self-respecting human beings. Today they were skin and bones, clad in striped blue and white prison uniforms with wooden shoes on their swollen feet. They no longer looked human. They wandered about among the piles of brick, rock and wet sand and toiled at their tasks. Whenever the guards were not looking, they would edge closer to our building, until they were directly under the windows. When we saw the "stripes" approaching, we would throw them down some bread.

What else did we have except the dry crusts which we denied ourselves? It was torture to see these shadows of people fling themselves on these crusts. They tore the crusts out of each other's mouths like dogs who have found a bone in a heap of garbage.

I can still see those starving prisoners in their striped uniforms fighting over the bread. This sight freezes the blood no less than that of women and children being led to slaughter. It was part of the Nazis' calculated plan to brutalize human instincts, to transform humans into beasts. I knew that my appearance was no different from those Jews while I was imprisoned in cell 258. Certainly a quick death was better than the endless pain of hunger.

Sabotage

We, the six Jewish bath attendants, were responsible for a series of acts of sabotage. We knew that we could not bring about the defeat of the army, but we could not overlook any opportunity to do the Germans even a small measure of harm.

The Germans used to bring large transports of items stolen from the dead: clothing, furs, bed linen, etc. They were of the highest quality and scheduled for shipment to Germany after the disinfection process. We saw to it that none of the material would be in fit condition for use by the enemy. On one occasion the chief of the Warsaw Gestapo brought us ten heavy sacks. They were sewn and sealed; we were under strict orders not to open them. The chief knew nothing about the disinfection process; I asked him if we should use hot steam or cold gas.

"Which is more effective?" asked the imbecile.

"The hot steam, of course."

"In that case, it's obvious what you should use. But it must be ready by tomorrow," he added.

"Jawohl," I agreed.

Naturally we suspected that these sacks must contain some very valuable merchandise. We ripped one open and found some expensive-looking furs. Our course of action was clear. Carefully, we sewed the sack back together and then proceeded to follow the instructions of the stupid Gestapo chief. After a ten-minute immersion in the hot steam, the furs would be reduced to small pieces of hard leather — they would crumble at the merest touch.

The next day the Gestapo chief picked up the sacks without ever looking inside. He was pleased with us and even gave us cigarettes.

We had a similar experience with a transport of a hundred down quilts. The hot steam turned the down into lumps as hard as rocks and as big as a fist. They even changed color in the process. Our only regret was that we couldn't be there when the Germans got ready to use them.

When we were sure that our operation was a success, we grew bolder and ruined almost everything that fell into our hands. The Jewish bath attendants of Pawiak performed their duties with the conviction that they were participants in the struggle against the enemy. They expected no appreciation, but even the Polish prisoners of Pawiak were grateful for our achievements. Since, in their eyes, the Jew remained an inferior creature no matter what his accomplishments, they thanked us in their own way: "You bath attendants are very decent Jew-boys!"

The "Information Bulletin," the underground

press of the London government, published in Warsaw during the German occupation, once printed an item about the good work of the Pawiak bath attendants. The Ukrainian guard, Barczenko (our watchman), brought us a copy of this issue. There we read: "The six bath attendants of Pawiak successfully fulfilled a civic obligation in the struggle against the occupying forces. They deserve the highest praise and recognition from all Polish freedom fighters."

At the time we were not at all happy with this notice. We regarded it as an example of journalistic irresponsibility. If the Gestapo heard of it, we would be the losers. For a long time we lived in fear. Fortunately, the Gestapo never did find us out.

Chapter 5

Security Personnel

Prison Guards — Gestapo Officials

The prison commandant was a young Prussian called Pietsch; we seldom saw him. Relying entirely on his deputies, he never interfered with the running of the prison. His staff was dependable and efficient. The two deputies who served under him during my stay in Pawiak were the most vicious and heartless sadists and murderers. When I came to Pawiak, Pietsch's deputy was the notorious Birkel (Bürkl). His very name struck terror in all of Warsaw. Birkel was sentenced to death by the Polish Underground and executed in August 1943. He was replaced by Forst, an old man who looked like an intellectual, but was a notorious thief and assassin by vocation. A sadist, he mistreated the prisoners at every opportunity.

The deputy commandant was surrounded by a dozen Gestapo officials, who were in charge of the various departments of the prison administration. Among them were: Alberts, Zanders and Doney. These men were on the prison grounds during the day only.

Prison Security

The prison patrol was a highly specialized operation consisting of eighteen people: six Germans and twelve Ukrainians. The changing of the guard took place at noon every day. Fruewirt, a waiter from

Vienna and a heartless creature, was the chief of the first patrol. Hanish, a half-Pole from East Prussia, was the chief of the second patrol. He was not as cruel as Fruewirt, and perhaps for that reason his men were also a little more lenient. When Hanish and his crew came on duty, we all breathed a little easier.

The Regime

Up until the summer of 1943 the prison regime was unconscionably rigid. The German and Ukrainian prison guards walked around in the corridor all day long, frequently peering into the cells through the small windows in the doors. If for any reason one of us displeased them, that prisoner was dragged out and tortured almost to death. Hundreds of prisoners were tortured every single day, by various methods. They were commanded to do "leap frog"; they were whipped and attacked by savage wolfhounds.

In the second half of 1943 the guards' cruelty abated somewhat. The number of individual tortures decreased, but at the same time, there was a substantial increase in executions of Poles. By that time it had become clear to everyone that a German defeat was imminent. The Ukrainians were the first to change their attitude toward us. By gaining our sympathy, they hoped to save their own skins in case of a military reversal. Some of them began to cooperate with the Polish Underground; others tried to atone for previous cruelty by treating the prisoners more kindly. This was the only reason for the more relaxed prison regime. But in all that time, treatment of Jews did NOT change. The Ukrainians as a group no longer tortured us, but the Austrian Fruewirt did not stop until the last moment.

The Other Members of the Prison Patrol

The other members of the patrol were prewar

The Executioners Have a Good Time ...

The first to the left is Kurt Nowotny, the murderer of the seven of the boiler room. The woman is the guard Marusia; she was executed by the Polish underground.

Polish prison guards — the so-called *Klawish*. There were twenty of them in Pawiak. A fraction of those who had served there before the war had volunteered to cooperate with the Germans. But still the Gestapo didn't trust them and gave them maintenance jobs. One *Klawish* was the cook in the kitchen; another was in charge of the boiler room; a third worked in the laundry, etc. Most of them behaved decently, but two of them plagued us. Oszewski, the foreman of the workshops, was a virulent anti-Semite responsible for the carnage of countless Jews. In the days of the ghetto, he had denounced many Jews hiding out on the "Aryan" side. Here he tortured and persecuted the Jewish artisans under his charge.

Another villain, nicknamed "Crazy Felus," a degenerate alcoholic, was chief of the boiler room. He harassed both Jew and Gentile workers and was responsible for the death of seven men who made a daring escape from the boiler room.

In conclusion, I must make mention of the "Volksdeutsch" female prison guards who had volunteered for this assignment. One of them, twenty-year-old Marusia, a prostitute by profession, specialized in the torture of Jewish women confined to the death chamber twenty-four hours before their execution. She forced them to crawl on all fours around the prison yard, tore out their hair and beat them.

No doubt Marusia also persecuted the Poles, because she was sentenced to death by the Polish Underground. The verdict was pronounced by the Polish fighters one evening in April 1944, on Koszykowa Street in the very heart of Warsaw. Marusia was lured into a dark doorway, the verdict was read to her and she was killed by a single bullet.

Another female prison guard whom the organization put to death was a forty-year-old woman. I knew who she was, but not by name. Every day she would stride through the prison yard just below our windows. She seemed like a well-bred, intelligent woman, but she turned out to be a provocateur. The women prisoners trusted her and gave her their *gryps* which she ostensibly took to the city. Instead, she turned them over to the Gestapo, thereby condemning hundreds of members of the Polish fighter organizations. She, too, met her death on a Warsaw street one beautiful spring day in 1944.

These were the tormentors and assassins who exercised unlimited power over thousands of human lives. In the last two years of Hitler's occupation of Poland a total of about forty thousand prisoners passed through the gates of this island of death, of this number approximately eight thousand Jews perished there without leaving a trace. Only a handful of the last Mohicans of the last Jewish community in Warsaw survived. They are dispersed around the world and, we hope, still alive.

Part II

PORTRAITS AND REFLECTIONS

Chapter 6

The Blond Hero

I remember the day distinctly — it was the latter part of July 1943. The morning was unusually hot; a heavy dampness lay oppressively on our hearts. In cell 258 the air was suffocating. We sat pressed close one to another, on our straw sacks. Hunger had robbed us of all strength.

The iron door was suddenly flung open. A handsome aristocratic-looking man entered the cell. Everyone jumped to his feet. The "newcomer" resembled no one we had ever seen in cell 258.

He stood for a moment by the door. Looking around, he said, "Oh, how hot it is in here!" And he threw off his elegantly-tailored jacket, cut in the latest Warsaw fashion, removed his shirt and, stripped to the waist, remained standing there in the middle of the cell.

We stared in disbelief at the well-built athletic body, the rippling muscles, handsome face and blond head of hair.

"Who are you? Are you Jewish?"

"Yes, I am a Jew and my name is Lifshitz although I haven't used that name in many years; I assumed a Polish name long before the war."*

The others murmured to each other: "He doesn't even look like a Jew, but they got him anyway."

* Lifshitz never disclosed his assumed Polish name. Perhaps he hoped that keeping it secret would save his family.

"How did you fall into their hands?"

Lifshitz started to talk fast, as if he wanted to share with us the awesome tragedy that had befallen him. He told us everything that had happened to him in the last twenty-four hours. We listened intently to his story:

Lifshitz appreciated the fact that he was one of the few fortunate Jews who had not spent even one day in the ghetto. Blond and blue-eyed, he did not look Jewish. Moreover, Lifshitz's well-to-do father had given his son a secular upbringing. Lifshitz went to the gymnasium (high school) and later to the university, where he studied chemistry. He was a good athlete as well; in his student year he had been one of the best swimmers and boxers of his circle. During his period of military service he acquired a reputation as the best marksman in his regiment. He was a favorite with his superior officers.

Upon his graduation from officers' school, Lifshitz began to think seriously about a career. During his army days he had made friends in Poznan. Now, with their help, he rented space in Poznan and opened a chemical supply store.

Poznan had always been an anti-Semitic city. Had Lifshitz revealed his Jewishness, he would not have had a single customer; small wonder that he posed as a Pole. Yet he married a Jewish girl from his home town with whom he lived happily until the war broke out. Not by word or deed did either of them ever betray their heritage, even to their closest neighbors. They assumed a new family name which sounded distinctly Polish.

Their pretense proved advantageous to them during the first years of the war. With the German occupation of Poznan, most of the Poles were driven out of the city. Like thousands of other Poles, Lifshitz, his wife and their small daughter settled in Warsaw. They did not need a new disguise. The inhabitants of Poznan knew them as Poles, and they easily continued to play the same role in Warsaw.

Lifshitz opened a small factory of chemical products and continued to make a good living; he even enlarged his plant. Although he carefully concealed his Jewish background, he never forgot who he was. As soon as he settled in Warsaw, he made contact with Jewish organizations; he supported Jewish causes. His factory became an underground center of the Jewish resistance movement, which laid the groundwork for the Warsaw Ghetto Uprising.

* * *

Today, Lifshitz awoke earlier than usual. Through sleep-filled eyes he glanced at the old wall clock which hung just opposite his bed. It was seven o'clock, golden sunbeams thrust boldly through the open window into his bedroom.

His wife and little daughter lay in the other bed still deep in slumber. His two-year-old son was sleeping in the small, woven straw crib. He had kicked off his blanket, turned himself around and straddled his bed.

Lifshitz slipped quietly out of bed. Barefooted, he walked over to the window and stood looking out on the quiet street. There were very few passersby. Far in the distance he heard the faint echo of the streetcar bell. Warsaw was enveloped in morning stillness. As he did every morning, Lifshitz performed his exercise routine. Then he washed, shaved and dressed quickly.

His wife awoke. She looked around the room sleepily. When she saw her husband, her face lit up with an affectionate smile, a smile of pleasure and boundless love. She admired him deeply: she knew that they were all alive today only because of his initiative and

81

superhuman strength. And she was sure that God would continue to protect them, until this nightmare ended.

Now she gazed at the tall, handsome, athletic figure of her husband. He walked over and sat down on the edge of her bed. She put her arms around his neck and kissed him. Lifshitz held her in his arms, kissing her tenderly. He said goodbye, kissed the sleeping children and quietly closed the door behind him.

Lifshitz went out into the street. As was his habit, he intended at first to ride to his factory. But today he seemd to have left earlier than usual. Since he was in no hurry, he decided to walk part of the way. He wanted to observe the activity and movement of the big city.

He strode along Marszalkowska Street. Throngs of Germans clad in uniform, or in civilian dress with swastikas in their buttonholes, walked nearby. Today he felt even more resentful than usual of these blackguards who strode through the vanquished city so arrogantly. At this hour there were many of them in the streets, hurring to their offices; some jumped into the streetcars marked "For Germans only."

Lifshitz stared at their fat, beefy faces and his heart overflowed with pain and loathing for the criminals who had slain millions of Jewish children. Suddenly he felt an irrepressible desire to spit into the face of a red-nosed high-ranking SS officer.

"Lifshitz, control yourself," he muttered under his breath.

Then, fast as a cat, he leaped onto a passing street-car.

He got out on Wolska Street. From there, he had only a short walk to his shop. Suddenly, aware that he was being followed, he turned his head. A tall man wearing high officers' boots was right behind him. His heart began to pound. Lifshitz was not a fearful person, but now he knew he was in danger. He quickened his steps and looked around for a way out. The street was almost empty, there was no place to hide from the pursuer. Should he run through a gate? At the same moment he decided it wasn't worth it. He knew all the gates in that neighborhood, and none of them had any passageways. They led nowhere, and he would be captured anyhow.

Now Lifshitz heard the rapid steps more distinctly. Two tall men appeared in front of him and a third came up from behind. One was holding a revolver, the other two had their hands in their pockets. They addressed Lifshitz in Polish, and he realized he was dealing with the *Kripo* (German criminal police, most of whose members were Polish). The one with the revolver, forcibly pushed Lifshitz into the nearest alley.

"Show us your documents, Jew," he ordered.

Lifshitz looked around him. He was standing pressed to the wall in a corner of a long alley. "It looks bad," he thought; trying to gain time, he answered the *Kripo* man's order with a question, "What do you want with my papers?"

Lifshitz thought he might be able to get away by offering them money, but the one with the revolver would not be bought off.

"Hands up!" he shouted.

Shaken to the core, Lifshitz hurled himself against the man with the revolver, his left hand gripping the hand that held the weapon. A quick twist and the gun began to slip from the *Kripo*'s grasp; Lifshitz seized it with his right hand. The agent was stunned; he had no time to catch his breath. The whole business took half a second; a shot was heard and the *Kripo* man lay on the ground. Another blast and the second man lay dead. Lifshitz pulled the trigger once more but the revolver was jammed. The third agent, whose life was

thus spared, began yelling for help. German gendarmes came running up, as though from nowhere.

* * *

"Headquarters of the Warsaw Security Police" read
the sign over the entrance to the huge building on
Szuch Avenue. On the second floor was a room
marked: "Jewish Division. In Charge: *Untersturm-
führer* (Second Lieutenant) Brand."

Lifshitz was taken into this room. Brand, a paun-
chy, benign-faced man of medium height, stood opposite Lifshitz. He already knew all about the incident
on Wolska Street. Now he looked at Lifshitz amicably
and with admiration. All he wanted to know was how
Lifshitz had managed to disarm the agent.

Lifshitz stood before Brand, trembling from head
to foot. He was convinced that there was no hope for
escape. He was not afraid of dying, but he knew the
Germans would torture him mercilessly because he
had killed two of their agents. Brand's friendly recep-
tion served to dispel his gloomy thoughts. Lifshitz
relaxed and showed Brand how he had seized the
weapon. Brand was delighted. He ran out of the
room and quickly returned with another Gestapo officer of slightly higher rank. Lifshitz had to demon-
strate his trick again. Then a great many more Gestapo officers came into the room; they looked at Lifshitz as though he were some kind of rare creature.
He had to perform several more times.

Finally, Brand slapped him warmly on the shoulder, patted his head and said, "You're a brave fellow.
We need young men like you in our ranks. You've got
nothing to be afraid of."

And with that, Brand ordered an excellent dinner
for Lifshitz, offered him cigarettes, and personally
escorted him, still with great courtesy, down to the
"streetcar" prison.

Lifshitz sat in the "streetcar" all by himself, reflecting on his situation. He could not imagine who had denounced him to the Nazis. He was astounded at how much they knew about him — everything, apparently, except his address. They even knew his original family name. Lifshitz felt trapped and wondered what would happen to him now.

His wife must be waiting for him: he always came home for dinner at this time. She would wait in vain, because he would not come home today. In fact, he might never see his wife and children again.

By now his wife would begin worrying because her husband was late. By evening, when he still had not returned, she would telephone the factory, just as she had done several weeks ago when he had come home late because of a business appointment. Except that time he had answered the telephone himself. Who would answer it today? Lifshitz was overwhelmed with pity for his wife and little children. Without him, he knew they would be completely lost. Oh, how cruel fate can be! He must sit here, a captive, and at home they were waiting for him . . . his, and Lifshitz whispered the word to himself, orphans.

Lifshitz spent an agonizing night, sitting in the big, wooden chair. In the morning a Gestapo officer took him from the cell and brought him back to Brand. The Gestapo chief received him with a broad smile, even asked him to sit down; he moved his own chair close to his. After inquiring how Lifshitz had spent the night and how he felt, Brand came to the point.

"As you know," he said quietly, "we don't want to harm you. You're a brave chap. I liked you the moment I set eyes on you. I want you to work for us. You'll help us ferret out these Polish bandits. You know damn well they haven't spared you Jews either. You know how much pain and misery you've had to put up with every day at the hands of these savages. And the agents who attacked you yesterday in the street were also Poles. Believe me, if it weren't for the Poles, we'd never lay a finger on you. We're doing it only because we are under pressure from those Polish bastards. If you accept my offer, you'll be fulfilling a patriotic Jewish duty."

Lifshitz sat there stunned. He had been prepared for any kind of offer but this one. For after all, what was Lifshitz now? One of many under sentence of death, and already in the hands of the enemy. He felt completely helpless. Why was Brand talking to him as though he were someone to be reckoned with, as though he had something which Brand wanted and needed? If Lifshitz had had enough time to consider the matter, he might have seen through Brand's duplicity. But Brand shrewdly insisted on an immediate answer.

"What is there to think about?" he urged him. "You should accept my offer. You know very well what you can expect if you refuse."

It had never crossed Lifshitz's mind to cooperate with the Germans against the Polish underground. He had worked on their behalf for many years and could never betray them. At that moment it became clear to him that Brand was lying. The Germans were not slaughtering masses of Jews because they wanted to triumph over the Poles. Agreed, the Poles are and were anti-Semitic, but all the same, they *were* at war with the Germans. For the time being, he, Lifshitz, and the Polish underground, had a common enemy; they were allies in the same cause. How could he ever dream of betraying his compatriots?

"I won't do it," he thought. Aloud, he asked, "Will you set me free?"

"Naturally," said Brand, but immediately qualified his answer. "If we have a guarantee that you won't run away."

Now Lifshitz had an idea. All he needed was a half

hour of freedom. There were many places to hide where the Germans would never find him. He would pretend to accept Brand's proposal.

"All right, I'll do as you say," he said in a dry voice.

"You've made a wise decision," Brand leaped out of his chair and elatedly slapped Lifshitz on the back. "I knew you had a good Jewish head on your shoulders. Smart fellow." Brand seemed overjoyed, as if the fate of Greater Germany, its ultimate victory depended on Lifshitz's decision.

Lifshitz's belief that the Gestapo was eager for his cooperation was now substantiated. He was filled with hope and joy. He would come out alive! Unconsciously, a smile appeared on his lips. Brand had been watching him all this time, and now he said, "What guarantee can you offer that you won't run away if we let you go?"

"I have a factory that is worth more than two million zlotys. Isn't that enough of a guarantee?"

Brand wasn't surprised. He shrugged his shoulders and said, "We know about your factory. But that isn't enough. If you want us to trust you, you must tell us where your family is. When we know that, we will be sure of you."

By this time Lifshitz was highly self-confident. The moment they let him go, he would hide out together with his family. Without thinking, he gave Brand his home address.

"Good. Now the matter is settled," said Brand calmly. "You'll be taken to Pawiak. You won't be too badly off, because I'll instruct the prison commandant to give you special privileges. You'll be detained in Pawiak no more than two days, just until we have proof that you've been telling us the truth. Then we'll send you out to work."

When Lifshitz mentioned that he had given Brand his home address, the veteran prisoners shrugged their shoulders and shook their heads, as though saying, "That was a mistake."

But Lifshitz didn't notice their reaction. He was sustained by the hope that he would soon be set free. He concluded his narrative, saying, "I won't be here more than a day or so. Brand has issued orders that I should be well treated. They didn't even search me. The German gave me cigarettes, but warned me not to give any to you."

Lifshitz promptly took a box of "Egyptians" from his pocket; eager to prove that he had no intention of obeying the prison guard, he lit a cigarette and passed it around for each of us to take a few puffs.

* * *

The sharp jingle of a bell pierced the morning silence. The prison night was over. A new day had begun: a new day of misery and suffering, torture and humiliation, hunger and want. The prisoners rubbed the sleep from their eyes. But the bell continued its obstinate summons, as though trying to wake the dead from eternal slumber. More than one prisoner sought to perceive in the sound of the bell what his fate would be, what this day would bring with it. For the one it might be liberation, for the other — death, for a third — the "transport," and for a fourth — a Gestapo interrogation, or torture in the prison.

Today there are thirty men confined to cell 258: twenty-four Jews and six Gypsies. The heat is unbearable, the fleas bite deep into our flesh with their burning needles; hunger gnaws and twists our guts. But there is no time to dwell on our anguish. We rise quickly, put on our tattered clothes, tidy the cell and form lines for roll call. After this routine, "breakfast" is brought in. The heavy door opens, and the bread is doled out. The loaves are small; each loaf is cut into four portions of 150 grams each.

Kazik the *Starosta* stands by the door to receive the

bread. Thirty portions means seven loaves and two extra slices. The entire operation proceeds with lightning speed. The Kapo hands the loaves to Kazik; he has no time to count them. A young Gypsy stands close beside him.

When the door is closed, Kazik counts the loaves. He has only six, plus the two separate portions; one loaf is missing. Kazik asks the Gypsy whether he has taken a loaf; the Gypsy denies it. How could he have taken the bread, there were other prisoners around him who would have seen him doing it. Apparently the Kapo made a mistake and counted six loaves instead of seven. Kazik opens the *Yudash* (peephole) and calls to the Kapo. The Kapo is a Polish prisoner; this one has never missed an opportunity to make trouble for the Jews. In spite of the tense atmosphere, Kazik reports the missing loaf to the Kapo. The Kapo knows nothing of course; he delivered the whole quota of loaves, he claims.

Everyone knows it is the Rat's turn of duty. Naturally the Kapo tells the Rat that "the Jews are complaining; they say they did not get enough bread."

The Rat enters the cell. "O.K. who took the bread?" he begins. Nobody confesses. The Rat flies into a rage and yells, "Now I'll show you! Everybody out!"

The prisoners of cell 258 stand in a row in the prison yard, facing the wall. We stand and wait. The Rat searches the cell, looking for the lost seventh loaf, which one of the inmates had stolen from his comrades.

Today the Rat's search is successful. Furious, he comes back into the yard, followed by two other prison guards; all three are armed with iron rods. The Rat approaches us and screams, "Down!"

The prisoners lie prone on the ground. The Rat raises his iron rod and shouts, "I'll teach you a lesson! You're hiding gold in the prison? Of course, I'm not surprised. Where there are Jews, there must be gold!"

For two hours, he forced us to crawl around the prison yard on all fours. Close behind came the Rat and the other two prison guards, beating us mercilessly with the iron rods. At the end of the two hours we were more dead than alive; we remained lying in the yard. The Rat gave orders to pour cold water on us until we got up.

Then he took us into a large room adjoining the administration office and held up two gold coins. "Which of you hid this money?" he asked.

Two young Gypsies confessed. Two days before the Germans had executed a great number of Jews in Pawiak.* After the execution the prisoners of cell 258 had been ordered to sort out and fold the clothing of the dead. The two young Gypsies had found the gold coins and hidden them. The affair of the "missing seventh loaf," also stolen by the Gypsies, led to the Rat's discovery of the gold coins.

I describe this episode mainly because of its direct bearing on our new cellmate Lifshitz. Lifshitz was among the group of unfortunate prisoners made to crawl on all fours in the prison yard. The prisoners saw *Oberscharführer* (chief barracks leader) Zanders emerge from the prison office, carrying a long whip. He came over to the group of Jews; it was obvious that he was on the lookout for someone. When he spotted Lifshitz, he walked over and flogged him with the whip, without respite. The other prisoners were so dazed by their own suffering that they were only partly aware of Lifshitz's extra ordeal. But later, while standing in the big room whose windows faced the prison gate, they were to witness the tragic epilogue to Lifshitz's story.

Zanders took Lifshitz to the prison gate; there Lifshitz could observe an automobile filled with Jews

* The Jews from the Hotel Polski

who were on their way to the ghetto ruins to be shot. In the van were Lifshitz's wife and two children. His baby son was sitting on his mother's lap. When the child saw his father, he cried out, "Papa! Papa!"

Lifshitz heard the voice of his son and the whole bitter truth flashed through his mind. He realized how he had been deceived. Brand had made a fool of him by wangling out of him his family's whereabouts. Now they were going off to their death. Clever Lifshitz, who thought that he could outfox Brand, was the victim of his own stupidity and naïveté. It was as if he had delivered his wife and children to the murderers with his own two hands.

The voice of his son made Lifshitz tremble from head to foot. Like a wild animal he pounced on Zanders. Before Zanders knew what was happening, he was flat on the ground with Lifshitz lying on top of him. Lifshitz seized the revolver from his holster.

But before he could aim the weapon and fire, several of the Ukrainian guards standing by the carload of Jews, ran over and began to beat Lifshitz over the head with their rifle-butts. They continued to beat him until Lifshitz lay motionless, soaked in blood.

The Ukrainians lifted the body from the ground, and tossed it into the automobile, which immediately started to move, escorted by a motorcycle squadron of white-uniformed gendarmes.

Chapter 7

Hauptscharführer Birkel (Bürkl)

When I hear descriptions of the type of German sadist who took pleasure in tormenting people, I see before me the face of the assistant commandant of Pawiak, *Hauptscharführer* Birkel. Birkel was notorious throughout Warsaw for his atrocities. The Polish underground press published in Warsaw frequently wrote about this beast in human disguise.

Birkel remains fixed in my mind: tall and lean, he held his head tilted somewhat to the right. His cold, grey eyes stared out at you from beneath the visor of the Gestapo cap. His nose was slightly bent, his lips pressed together and grim. He paced about the prison yard like a demon. If his gaze happened to fall upon a prisoner not doing his job the way he thought he should, Birkel would pounce on him. He used to torture his victims to death.

Birkel had two wolfhounds, whom he himself had trained in the art of cruelty. These dogs followed him around in his tours of inspection around the prison yard. I cite a typical scene in Pawiak during Birkel's regime: In the midst of a deathly silence, Birkel comes striding through the yard with firm steps, the echo of his iron-studded boots resounding in the silence. Close behind, jaws pointing down and tails between their legs, slink the hounds; Rolf, the bigger of the two, followed by Dina — smaller, but no less dangerous. The trio advances slowly; when Birkel spots a prey whom he is too lazy to deal with himself, he directs the hounds, "Go get him!"

The dogs leap on the man. Rolf, the stronger one, throws him to the ground; then both beasts proceed to eat their victim up alive. They tear out chunks of flesh, howling savagely when they smell blood. The victim gives a fearful cry of pain; the dogs growl and snarl. Birkel stands by, watching with a pleased smile.

With fatherly affection he strokes the beasts' necks, "Brave boys! Good dogs!" The warm blood still dripping from their jaws, the dogs are taken by Birkel into the prison bathhouse to be washed.

Left to his own devices, Birkel would never have differentiated between Polish or Jewish prisoners: to him they were all inferior beings. But he did have to abide by certain regulations as far as Polish prisoners were concerned. He could not torture a Pole without good reason, whereas a Jew could be punished at will.

I witnessed two such gruesome spectacles. Block Three of the prison was set aside for Poles accused of major political transgressions against the Nazis. The Germans treated these captives with special attention. One time, the prison guard of this block, having found some cigarettes in one of the cells, reported the infraction to the barracks leader. The latter immediately showed up in Block Three to "discipline" the guilty ones. Then Birkel appeared and took them down to the prison yard. The prisoners saw the huge piles of smoldering embers which had been removed from beneath the boilers just minutes before: they were still blazing hot. Dense, suffocating smoke rose from the piles and blotted out the sunlight from the entire area. Birkel made the prisoners form a circle; he ordered them to take off their shoes and jump barefoot onto the glowing embers. For half an hour these poor souls were forced to jump on and off the blazing piles. When they were finally released, all the participants in this "athletic show" had suffered severe burns; several died.

Birkel arranged another sadistic spectacle, this time with a group of Jews. Fifteen Jews had been picked up on the "Aryan" side and brought to Pawiak. Like all Jews taken into custody, they were spiritually broken: they knew that tomorrow they would be dead. Birkel decided to amuse himself with this group. He approached them and announced affably: "You're going to take a bath." Whereupon he escorted them to the prison bathhouse, told them to undress and stand under the shower. Then he ordered the bath attendants to run the boiling water. The attendants stood by thunderstruck, unable to move. The oldest attendant gathered his courage and said, *"Herr Hauptscharführer*, I must respectfully call to your attention that these people will be scalded."

Birkel took out his revolver, placed it at the attendant's face and fired at the ceiling. Seeing all the attendants trembling with fear, he screamed, "I'll shoot you all down, you shit bags! Didn't you hear my orders? You," pointing the gun at the head of the oldest orderly, "will you or will you not turn on the water?"

Birkel's nostrils twitched with rage, sparks flew from his eyes. The bath attendant had no choice but to obey. With stumbling steps he walked over to the water-apparatus and with trembling hands turned on the water. Birkel stood beside the attendant his eye riveted on the thermometer. All the while he kept his revolver in his hand, threatening the Jews who were standing under the scalding downpour: "Nobody move! Whoever moves, gets a bullet!"

The Jews emerged from under the shower covered with red, brown and blue blisters. Birkel yelled: "One minute to get dressed! Out!"

The severely burned Jews were unable to get

dressed. They grabbed the garment nearest to hand and stumbled naked out of the bath.

* * *

I saw that incident with my own eyes, and although by that time we had grown accustomed to all kinds of atrocities, the scene of these people being boiled alive nearly finished me. After I regained my composure I reflected upon the power of the human instinct of survival. Those fifteen Jews had been in no doubt regarding their fate. They knew that tomorrow they would be dead anyway. Why then did they allow Birkel to torture them today? True, Birkel threatened them with immediate death. But their death was inevitable ... What was the difference if they were killed by a bullet from Birkel's revolver *today*, or were taken by auto to the execution side on Zamenhof 19 *tomorrow*? On the contrary, if they had been felled by Birkel's shot here, on the spot, they could have saved themselves the excruciating road to the gallows. But the condemned Jews did not react with logic: they paid a high price for those few extra hours of life.

A few days later Birkel himself came up against the force of the instinct for survival. By August 1943 everyone in Pawiak knew that the Polish Underground had sentenced Birkel to death. I am sure that Birkel was aware of it too, but he could not bring himself to believe that death would dare touch him.

By chance I met Birkel one morning towards the end of August. He was taking his two dogs to the bathhouse, and had given orders to the attendants to wash them. But this time Birkel controlled himself; he treated us politely, even courteously.

One of the bath attendants working with us at the time was a Polish lad named Zbyszek Skibinski. He was about seventeen years old. Seeing that Birkel was in a good mood, the boy approached him and said, "*Herr Hauptscharführer*, I have a watch in the prison vault. Timepieces are necessary for our work here. I request permission to have the watch returned to me."

We all waited with bated breath, amazed at the boy's audacity. What would happen now?

To our astonishment Birkel replied calmly, "O.K., you'll get your watch."

Birkel promptly made out a claim slip to have the watch returned to Zbyszek. Then he thanked us all for washing his dogs and left. While he was still with us, I could not help staring at this beast; he was calm, didn't show a trace of fear.

That very evening he was shot to death on a Warsaw street by the Polish Underground.

Chapter 8

Alberts – The Angel of Death

The Slaughter of "American" Jews

In the summer of 1943, "Jewish Warsaw" was a pile of rubble. The ghetto had been destroyed, its inhabitants slaughtered or poisoned in the gas chambers of Treblinka and Majdanek.

Thousands of Jewish refugees from the ghetto who had managed to escape now found themselves homeless on the "Aryan" side. Some were hiding in holes and dark corners; others wandered about the streets, more often than not without a place to spend the night. Some of them still had some money, but they knew no one willing to help them to find a shelter. Most of them were betrayed by their Jewish faces and even more by the sadness in those Jewish eyes — a sadness which reflected the suffering of their people's fate. The vast majority were penniless and without friends among the Poles; their situation was the worst. But all of them, without exception, could at any moment fall into enemy hands.

The Gestapo was able to exterminate hundreds of these refugees by means of a hoax, labelled, curiously enough *South American Documents*. The Gestapo had a list containing names of those Jews who had permits to emigrate to the Americas and those for whom permits had been requested by relatives already living in Latin America. One day an office was opened in the Hotel Polski for the purpose of registering these Jews.

News of the new office spread rapidly and aroused great excitement among the refugees. At first people were skeptical, but they went anyway. And no wonder! Many of them were homeless; Hotel Polski was their only hope of salvation. Others followed; one drew the other. Unfortunately, some of those who were lured to the hotel would have been able to survive on the "Aryan" side, for they had good hiding places and authentic papers.

Hotel Polski hummed with activity. In a short time the first transport of Jews, the "South American Citizens," was sent out. The Germans saw to it that this group sent favorable reports to their friends in Warsaw. Soon it was learned that the Jews were at a camp in Vittel — a health resort in France — where they were waiting to be exchanged for German citizens in the Americas. They were well treated, in fact were enjoying the best of everything. How wonderful! After years of misery and anguish in the ghetto, after an insecure and hazardous existence on the *Aryan* side, a sojourn in a spa seemed like a dream.

In the meantime, a "committee" was set up in the Hotel Polski. Its Jewish organizers included Zurawin, Lolek, Skosowski, and Kenigl. They were assisted by Jews and Poles whose job it was to recruit candidates for emigration. Every day dozens of Jews paid many thousands of zlotys for the privilege of having their names added to the "American" list. They brought with them to Hotel Polski whatever belongings they had been able to salvage, including jewelry and cash. The Jews enjoyed life in the hotel. They ate, drank their fill, played bridge, and, in general, felt as though life was starting anew. They felt confident that the bad times were over. The Germans did nothing to shatter this illusion. In the salons of the hotel, Gestapo agents chatted amiably with the Jews and distributed cigarettes. This "idyll" lasted until mid-

July 1943: Hotel Polski had fulfilled its role. German police encircled the hotel and all the "guests" were taken off to Pawiak.

* * *

Obersharführer Alberts was chief of Pawiak's household personnel; he occupied an important position in the administrative office. Every prisoner eventually got to know this elegant Gestapo officer. Alberts considered himself a very handsome man. His main ambition was to set a prime example as a Nordic man, a member of the "Glorious Herrenvolk."

At first, the tall, erect figure of *Obersharführer* Alberts made a favorable impression on us. It was some time before we could judge him more objectively.

Wearing gloves and boots rubbed to a high polish, he made his rounds through the prison yard, several times a day. He held his head high and strode with firm, military step. We never heard Alberts raise his voice at anyone or beat anyone. When other Gestapo officers encountered one of us, they pretended not to see us. But Alberts was different. He always acknowledged the prisoner's timid salutation with a gracious, courteous gesture of the hand.

The Jewish inmates of cell 258 knew that every morning, punctually at ten, Alberts paid his daily visit to neighboring cell 257, the Jewish death cell. We also knew that Alberts escorted the condemned men to the prison's administrative office and from there to the "Umsiedlung" (execution). The Jews of cell 258 had a special name for kind and courteous Alberts: they dubbed him "The Angel of Death." Some maintained that this tall functionary of the prison guard was killing Jews with his own hands. None of us believed these allegations. Executions were the duty of the "white gendarmes": what need was there for Alberts to participate? He had his staff of reliable, dependable murderers. If Alberts *was* participating in the killings himself, he must be doing so of his own volition, for the sadistic pleasure it afforded him.

"It's not possible," we argued among ourselves, "that the genteel and polite Alberts could be such a vicious sadist. He is what he is, we know that, but the rumors about him must be exaggerated."

But the artisans of Block Four (a group I subsequently joined) told a different story. From their windows, they commanded a clear view of the site opposite the prison gate. It was here, amidst the devastated buildings of Dzielna 25 and 27 that the executions of the "Umsiedlung" Jews were often carried out. The artisans frequently saw Alberts fire his automatic at the victims. The evidence was too overwhelming. Alberts was guilty.

Now that we had seen through him, the mere echo of his footsteps could make us tremble. I had a concrete example of his sadism much later on when, together with my five comrades, I worked in the prison bathhouse.

One morning Alberts appeared outside the open window of the bathhouse. In his usual calm and courteous manner he asked, "How many of you are working here?"

"Six," one of us replied.

"All Jews?"

"Jawohl!"

"Everybody out!" he ordered.

We exchanged glances: "This is the end." If Alberts, the "Angel of Death," had come for us, could there be any doubt about our fate?

Shaking with fear, we went out of the bathhouse. Alberts told us to form a line. We obeyed, and tried coming to terms with the thought of death. But Alberts was in no hurry; he counted us slowly, looking at us with his enigmatic smile. He was a poor mathematician! There were six of us, but he had to do a recount. It seemed to take forever; one could have tallied a whole army division in that time.

But time was never the issue in Pawiak. While we watched, Alberts pulled something out of his pocket. To our amazement, it was a box of cigarettes. He opened it, and gave each of us three cigarettes. Then with that familiar gesture of his hand, he turned on his heel and left. We remained rooted to the spot.

"What was that all about?" we asked each other. Later we found out that Alberts had returned from leave that day, and was handing out three cigarettes to every prisoner with an assigned "job." We would gladly have done without Alberts' form of greeting, and willingly have forfeited even the much coveted cigarettes.

* * *

It is late afternoon in mid-July; the day has been very hot. The air in our basement cell in Block Eight is, as usual, oppressive and damp. Our shirts stick to our bodies. It is more crowded than ever because of three new arrivals. We are so weak that we can hardly talk. Even the younger ones sit in silence, too exhausted to carry on their usual arguments.

Suddenly we heard a whirring noise coming through our cell window: automobiles drive into the prison yard. A violent commotion follows, then a jumble of loud outcries in German, and the barking of dogs.

We were not accustomed to such an uproar in the prison yard. Kazik, the *Starosta*, pushed a small bench to the wall under the window, climbed up and looked out, keeping to one side of the window to avoid being seen. After a short while he jumped off and reported: "Quite a crowd out there; I can tell they are Jews. The women are well dressed and are carrying a lot of luggage, expensive valises. There are children also."

101

"What can it be?" we wondered. There must have been an "Action" somewhere.

Litwak, a young prisoner from Warsaw, ran over to the bench and took a turn looking out. He reported: "They must have liquidated Hotel Polski. I know all those people; I was with them until yesterday morning. They caught me at the back door of the hotel, just as I was going out to help a friend go down into the sewer — that was the only way back to the ghetto now; he had some money stashed away there and insisted on getting it. Now they've rounded up all the other Jews who were in the hotel. Yes," he concluded gloomily, "that's over with, too."

The tiny window became an observation post to the courtyard. Cautiously we stood and watched the proceedings in the prison yard. A throng of men, women and children stood lined up in rows. Their belongings lay piled up to one side. Two Gestapo officials, Brand the mass murderer of Warsaw Jews, and his assistant, Mende, sat at a long table in the exact center of the yard. Beside them stood several Gestapo prison guards, headed by *Oberscharführer* Alberts.

Brand, with his bloated, beefy face, was in charge of the proceedings. One after the other he ordered the Jews over to the table. After examining their documents, he sent some to the left and others to the right. The line on the left grew larger and larger; the one on the right never exceeded a few dozen people.

There was no doubt about it — this was a "selection." To people who were not subjected to the German rule in Poland, this term may have no special significance. But to those of us who went through this hell, this seemingly innocent word evokes terror and horror. During and after the "selections," millions of Jews were massacred in Poland.

The Gestapo had evidently come to the conclusion that there was no point in continuing the Hotel Polski

game. The Gestapo had won easily; they had succeeded in luring a number of Jews into the trap. The
first groups which had been sent to Vittel or Hanover
were no better off either: they were still in Gestapo
hands under constant observation; no one could save
them. It was high time to bring the situation in Warsaw to a close.

I stood for a long time on the small bench alongside
the tiny window of my cell, watching the march of
death. Had I been caught looking out, the Germans
would have immediately fired at me. But I was convinced that I had only a few more days to live and
gave no thought to the danger. I could not tear myself
away from the spectacle. The sight of the children,
especially, sent a shudder through me. Children —
some bigger, some smaller, with blond heads, rosy
faces, their eyes darting back and forth, clinging to
their mothers, trembling. Yes, I saw them all trembling, for they must have had an inkling of where
they were and what was happening.

In that moment, I saw in my mind's eye the face of
my own little daughter who, only a short time ago at
another "selection," had perished the same way.

The Germans proceeded about their task with their
usual efficiency. Once the papers were examined, the
victim was dismissed. I knew what these lines meant:
the left side was death, the right was life — or, rather,
a temporary reprieve.

The selection went on until late into the night.
Then all those people were herded into the prison
and the iron gate slammed shut behind them. The
noise of hundreds of pairs of running feet resounded
in our corridor. The small group of Jews from the
right line were taken to the women's section; the
throng from the left was driven into our section, the
section of death.

Through our closed door we could hear the captives being driven into the cells. Soon after came the deathly hush of a night in Pawiak.

The next morning the "selection" group was ordered out of the cells and back into the corridor where they were told to form a line for their breakfast-coffee. A group of women happened to be standing outside the door of our cell; we tried to engage them in conversation. The lame Czaryski addressed them through the round observation window in the door.

"What's happening with you?"

"We are done for," a small, dark-haired woman answered him in Yiddish. "We're being sent down there," she pointed to the floor.

The line moved forward. Ukrainian guards approached, and we couldn't talk anymore.

Several hours later there was another tumult in the corridor. Once more the people were driven out of their cells, and ordered to form lines. They stood in a double line, stretching along the entire hundred meters of the corridor. Then they were sent into the yard in groups of five. A short time after the first group was outside a loud salvo of gunfire could be heard. The executions had begun.

Soon another group of women was standing outside our door. But we couldn't look out anymore. I could hear a woman sobbing, and then another woman chiding her, "Stop crying, you little fool. We can only die once. Try to control yourself. Don't give *them* the satisfaction of breaking down."

* * *

When I was transferred to Block Four, my friends gave me a detailed account of this execution — the Jews of Block Four could see everything from their windows: Carrying long sticks, the Ukrainian guards drove naked people, five at a time, from the prison gate, along the empty street, until they reached the devastated area just opposite Pawiak gate, the ruins of Dzielna 25 and 27.

The Ukrainian guards then chased their victims to a small wooden bridge suspended over a deep excavation. The moment they set foot on the bridge they were cut down by machine gun fire and they tumbled into the pit below.

Thus they marched in groups of five, one group after another — men, women and children. Looking in the direction from where the shots were coming, one of the observers spotted a figure standing in the shadows of the demolished wall. He recognized Alberts — the "Angel of Death." He stood erect as ever, his hands, still encased in snow white gloves, grasping a machine gun. Each time a group of naked Jews set foot on the bridge, Alberts would raise the automatic; the shots rang out. Then, with the same graceful gesture with which he always greeted us in the prison yard, he lowered the weapon. That day, Alberts massacred three hundred people single-handed. Among the dead were women and children; many of them were buried alive.

Chapter 9

My "Friend" Willie

I met him in 1943. Although it was already late autumn, winter that year delayed its cold embrace; Warsaw was enjoying sunny, balmy days.

I was sitting near the entrance to the prison bathhouse, next to my disinfection cauldron, thinking, as I always did, about the fate of my family, my own situation and the hopeless future. Someone knocked on the door; it was a rule of the prison that our door must always remain closed. The Ukrainian prison guard had the key, and he opened the door. Three men entered, wearing the striped uniforms of the concentration camp, with blue berets on their heads. They were German non-Jewish inmates of the concentration camp on Gesia Street.

Since the camp had no bathing facilities, they had come to us. The first of the trio, a tall, blond man with the face of an intellectual, attracted my immediate attention. He walked right over to me, pressed my hand and said,

"My name is Willie. I keep the records in the camp hospital. The other man is the camp doctor and the third one is the administrator. You know what I mean, a kind of 'factotum.'"

"I understand," I replied, and greeted them all.

Then came the routine questions that all prisoners ask whenever they meet anyone new. "How much longer? When will our misery be over?"

The answer usually came in the form of another question. "Who knows?"

But Willie's response was different; he was convinced that our ordeal would soon be over. "The Soviets are making giant strides on all the fronts. They're very close to the former Polish borders. They should be in Warsaw in a matter of weeks." Willie assured me that the Russians were our only chance for salvation.

Willie told me all about himself. He has been a prisoner from the time of Hitler's advent to power in 1933. Formerly a lawyer in Berlin, he was an active social democrat; his arrest came about because of his political activism. In the ten years of his confinement, he had been in many concentration camps, undergone much anguish and torture. Now he was locked up in "Concentration Camp Warsaw." Conditions there were not too bad, but the eleventh year of detention had seriously undermined his health.

"The Gestapo has accused me of major political crimes," he explained. "I have no hopes of coming out alive. I know that when their own end draws near, they'll finish me off. I *must* try to escape."

After this first meeting we saw Willie almost daily. Because of his work in the hospital, he had to bathe often. Once, as we sat side by side, I asked him to tell me about his family.

"I have a wife and two children in Berlin," he told me. "At first we were able to communicate with each other and we would exchange letters once a month. Later on my family renounced me. I don't want any part of them. I never want to see them again. If I do survive these terrible days, I'll settle in South America and write a book about everything I saw and experienced during my eleven years in the Nazi concentration camps."

One day two young Germans — inmates of the

same camp on Gesia Street — made their escape; they fled to the Prussian frontier, hoping to cross it and find their way home. But they were captured by the border police. This time, they were sent to Pawiak and placed in solitary confinement to await the gallows: according to Nazi rules, escapees inevitably ended up on the gallows. I met these two young men once, when they came to bathe. They insisted that Himmler himself would pardon them and that they would survive. They asked me to tell Willie to send cigarettes and food to their cell.

When I gave Willie this message, he said, "You know, if it were up to me, I would try to get them what they asked for; those boys need it badly. But our friends in the camp resent them. First of all, they are angry because those fellows chose the wrong moment for their getaway. A lot of us were supposed to get passes to go into town, and they spoiled our chances. Do I have to tell you that such a pass can be the road to freedom? Moreover, they fled to Germany, and we German political prisoners consider this to be an act of treason. Everyone of us has blotted out memories of our ungrateful Motherland; we never want to lay eyes on her again. After Hitler's defeat we plan to march throughout Poland wearing our striped uniforms. Everyone will see that *we* do not belong to the ranks of the persecutors, but to the persecuted victims, just like all of you."

I believe implicitly that Willie was one of us. We, the six bath attendants, always welcomed him with open arms, sharing with him whatever we had, confiding to him all our secrets.

Together with Willie we worked out an escape plan. It hinged on the fact that once a week all the inmates of the concentration camp on Gesia Street came to us to bathe. An unending stream of hundreds of striped uniforms swarmed in and out of the prison gate;

amidst this chaos the prison guards could not possibly keep track of everyone. While one group of "stripes" was bathing, we planned to go into the next room and exchange clothes with them. Then we and Willie, together with a large group of camp prisoners, led by an SS officer whom we would bribe, would walk out through the prison gate under the very eyes of the guard.

Once in the ghetto, our group, still with Willie, would take off — a race through the ghetto area, a jump over the wall, and we would be in the city. Naturally, we obligated ourselves to take Willie along with us and find him, as well as ourselves, a hideout in Warsaw.

The plan seemed workable, with good chances of success. There were only two obstacles: what to do with our Ukrainian prison guard, and how to find an SS officer in the camp on Gesia willing to lead us out of prison.

The two Ukrainian guards working in the bath house were not on duty together: one worked the first shift and the other the second; they alternated every other day. Barczenko was a true friend, a decent Gentile whom we could never involve in such a dangerous undertaking. But Kostienko, the second one, was a different matter. Before coming to Pawiak, he had been trained in a special SS school and taught the fine "arts" of cruelty. He had been well-trained. For example: revolver in hand, he would stand quietly in a corner of the prison yard; unseen by anyone, he would survey the barred windows. If he spotted the head of a prisoner, who merely longed for a breath of fresh air, or a view of the outside world, he would promptly take aim. As luck would have it, Kostienko was as rotten a shot as he was a human being. He usually missed; only once did he kill an inmate.

It was in the bathhouse that Kostienko displayed his prowess. He persecuted and molested the bath attendants to his heart's content. And as if that were not enough he harassed the prisoners whose turn it was to bathe. I saw Kostienko and an SS guard drag out an elderly Viennese Jew and then beat him with their steel whips; they did not stop until their victim was half dead. Kostienko had ordered one of us to hold the victim: our comrade refused, so we all received a whipping later on.

It was part of our plan to teach Kostienko a lesson. By throwing him into the disinfection cauldron and sealing the top, we would render him harmless. There was every chance that he would suffocate; in any event, he would not be able to sound the alarm. The first stumbling block was removed.

For the rest, we had to depend on Willie. He assured us that he could easily find an SS officer to lead us to safety. In the course of our plotting, we found out that Willie had no decent suit of clothes to wear. What's more, he had no shoes and no overcoat. Showing up in the city in prisoner's stripes would be courting immediate arrest. What, then, was to be done? We got together. One of us gave Willie a pair of pants, the other a jacket, the third a coat and a pair of shoes. Now he looked presentable and we could continue with preparations for our escape.

Willie thought there was no time to lose. "We must be out of here no later than the end of 1943," he warned us. Here it was the end of November already. Naturally we agreed with him, for every day only brought fresh dangers. The sooner we got out the better.

One day Willie introduced me to *Sturmmann* Mut, the prison guard who escorted his group to the bathhouse. "He's on our side," Willie confided. "He's an old-time Socialist; you can tell him anything you want. I'll try to convince him to help us get out of here."

I engaged Mut in conversation. He told me politely that although he would like to help us, as chief of the guards in the concentration camp, he was in no position to do so. He promised to find us another SS man.

Several days later Willie introduced us to a Rumanian Volksdeutsch. Immediately we set about discussing with him the details of our escape. But then disillusionment began to set in. One afternoon Mut was sitting with us. He was very drunk and in a jovial mood; he began bragging about his great exploits of the day before. He had been escorting a group of Greek Jews to their job in the ghetto. (We knew these Jews: many had swollen feet, and every day more were dying from ailments related to their famished condition.)

While Mut was with them, three of them had slipped away to forage in the ghetto ruins for something to eat.

"Can you imagine the nerve of those lousy Jews?" Mut went on cheerfully. "I was very annoyed and went to look for them. I found them in a ruined cellar. What do you think I did?" Mut's gray eyes shone and his face was distorted. "I shot them on the spot, those 'shit-heads'! With this!" and he pointed to his revolver.

I thought, "A drunkard tells the truth. But how could a Social Democrat, a man that Willie assured us was one of us, do such a thing? Something was indeed wrong!" I kept quiet, and let Mut talk, but I felt very uneasy.

A short time later my fellow bath attendants were treated to a firsthand lesson in the ethical values of Mut's brand of Social Democracy. Relying on Mut's promised help, two of our friends, Finkelstein and Chill, gave him letters to take to their acquaintances in

Warsaw. In the letters they asked for money. Mut delivered the letters, but kept the money he received for himself: the prisoners never saw any of it.

The second disappointment was Willie himself. He suddenly stopped coming to see us. We were terribly upset; all our hopes for escape were bound up with him. Then we found out that Willie had become a big shot in the camp; he was given an exit pass and could go to Warsaw every day. Everything began to make sense. With his permit, Willie was free to choose the time of his escape. He didn't need us anymore — of what use were six poor Jews to him now?

Thus ended our dream of freedom.

Worse yet, we learned that with Willie's rise to power, he had taken to torturing his fellow prisoners; indeed, Jews were singled out as his prime targets.

Now that Willie felt secure and firmly entrenched he gave up all thoughts of escape. But his reign did not last long. He contracted typhus and spent several months in the Pawiak hospital; there he was frequently visited by the camp commandant, a Gestapo *Sturmbannführer*. Willie recovered and returned to the camp shortly before the Warsaw Uprising in August 1944.

Willie's plans to march through Poland in his striped uniform never materialized. Nor did his plan to settle in America to write memoirs of the Nazi concentration camps. Willie is dead. After the liberation, I heard the story from a Pawiak survivor, a man who participated in the uprising. Willie was among the handful of German inmates still in the Gesia St. camp at the outset of the revolt. The Nazis dressed these prisoners in SS uniforms: Willie became an official member of the SS. Together with his "fellow officers" he defended the camp against the Polish insurrectionists. But the camp was overrun by the Poles during the first attack; Willie was killed together with his SS comrades.

Chapter 10

One of the Bravest

At the beginning of my internment in cell 258 — in fact, the same morning of our friend Lifshitz's arrival — another newcomer was added to our group. He was a man in his early twenties, tall and dark haired, with a distinctly Jewish face. He was dressed in dark breeches and high officers' boots, a blue summer shirt and a yellow jacket. In his hand he held a composition book and an unsharpened pencil. We were so engrossed in Lifshitz's story that we didn't notice the newcomer. All except Mardeks, the seventeen-year-old Hassid, who exclaimed, "Just look who's here! This fellow must think he's in school! He's got a notebook and a pencil!" Mardeks laughed aloud, but still nobody paid attention.

Only at evening roll call, when we found out that the newcomer belonged to the "plus" category, did we become curious. It was strange. What was a "plus" doing here, when he should be in cell 257? We cross-examined him.

"Are you a Jew?"

"If I said I wasn't, would you believe me?"

"What's your name?"

"Heniek Lederman."

"Where do you come from?"

"From Warsaw. My father was a tanner. We had a leather-dyeing business."

"Why the notebook and pencil?"

"The Gestapo officer at Szuch Avenue gave them to me and told me to write down everything about the apartment where the Germans had nabbed me."

Lederman had fought in the Warsaw Ghetto Uprising on Franciszkanska Street, not far from the ghetto walls on Bonifraterska. The night before the Germans surrounded the ghetto — the eve of Passover — Heniek was ordered to his post by the fighter organization, he promptly hid his wife and child in a nearby bunker and took up his position.

For several days he was engaged in furious combat.

During all this time he could not stop thinking of his wife and child. At one point, he was able to break away and make his way to the building where they were hidden in a bunker. There was no trace of the building — the entire area was devastated, the houses reduced to rubble and the cellars blocked up. All night Heniek dug in one of the cellars where he thought the bunker was. When he finally uncovered the bunker it was empty. Not a living soul was to be found. To this day, Heniek has no idea what happened to his family and the other people who were hiding there.

Late that same night Heniek returned to his combat group and resumed the struggle. By that time the Jewish insurgents had lost their entrenched positions. The Germans had burned down most of the ghetto and Jews had to look for hiding places in the ruins. During the day they remained out of sight; at night they roamed the ghetto foraging for food and attacking the Germans whenever possible.

Except for sporadic, short-lived shooting, the ghetto was quiet. The Germans, evidently, had quelled the rebellion. During the day Heniek lay hidden among the ruins; he saw armed Germans, accompanied by bloodhounds, roaming about on the lookout for the last remaining Jewish survivors in the bunkers. Jews of the *Befehlstelle* helped the Germans in this "search and destroy" action. Because of their invaluable assistance to the Germans in this task Heniek held the *Befehlstelle* Jews in the greatest contempt; to him they were the most despicable of traitors. "We despised them to such a degree," he said, "that we killed them wherever and whenever we could."

Heniek was still together with his small combat group, now down to eight youngsters. They knew they could not hold out much longer — they were out of ammunition. So they tried to escape from the ghetto through the sewers but the Germans discovered their route and tossed hand grenades into the sewer opening. Heniek suffered only a superficial leg wound; but he could not find any of his comrades.

Now he was all alone. He wandered about these unfamiliar underground passages for several days. One night, when he could stand it no more, he climbed out and found himself once more in the ghetto. Again he hid out in the ruins. He made several more attempts to reach his way to the "Aryan" side by ways of the sewers; on the night of July fourth he finally succeeded.

"I landed somewhere in the old section of the city," Heniek went on. "I had some Polish friends in Warsaw, good friends, and I asked one of them to hide me. Although it was not an easy matter, in my penniless condition, my friend did not refuse. The only place I could find without bribing anyone was an apartment which served as a secret arsenal for the Polish underground. But, as it turned out, the Nazis were on to it by now. My occupancy came to an abrupt end only three days after I moved in. I was enjoying a relaxing game of cards with the Polish army officer with whom I shared the flat when a loud knock was heard at the door. The officer jumped up, ran to the window and looked out. 'We are surrounded.'

"It was too late to run away. At the last moment the officer seized a hand grenade, but the Germans had already flung open the door; we could see the green helmets of the gendarmerie. The Pole hurled the grenade at them. There was a loud explosion, a dense cloud of smoke mixed with plaster enveloped the room. We heard desperate screams, muffled by the sound of shots. When the smoke cleared, I saw the Polish officer standing under the wall, his automatic sptting fire. The gendarmes were shooting from the door. I had no firearms: I could only stand and watch.

"The whole confrontation lasted several minutes. When it was over, the Polish officer lay on the ground. But, there were also three dead gendarmes in the foyer all slain by his grenade.

"The Germans grabbed me, and took me to the Gestapo. Knowing that I was lost, I confessed everything, withholding only the name of the friend who had brought me to this hiding place. The Gestapo officer gave me this pad and pencil. I am under orders to write a detailed report about the arsenal. So that's why I'm here with this school equipment," Heniek concluded.

"You must write very slowly," one of the older cellmates advised him. "Because when you're finished they won't need you any more. You know what they do with Jews."

Several weeks after Heniek's arrival I was able to make my getaway from cell 258. As I mentioned before, fate had hurled me from cell 258 into the camp on Gesia Street. After eleven days of anguish, I returned to Pawiak, but not to cell 258. I became a "plus" and was confined to #257, the death-cell. I knew now that I had reached the final stage of my ordeal. I was ready; death no longer frightened me. I felt that life was not worth fighting for.

In cell 257 were about a dozen other convicted Jews recently brought here from Warsaw. Among them was Heniek Lederman.

I was brought to the death cell on Saturday morning. Sunday being a day of rest, the execution would be postponed until at Monday at dawn. Although I was prepared for death, I welcomed the prospect of two more days of life.

I was exhausted, drained of strength. I had not eaten for twenty-four hours. I sat down on the edge of the straw pallet, waiting for the food to be brought. Heniek moved over beside me.

"Why are you so depressed?" he asked.

"I'm hungry. I haven't eaten since yesterday morning and I'm very weak."

"They'll soon be bringing our dinner soup. Don't worry, friend, they won't kill us now."

"How do you know?" I asked in surprise.

"I've been sitting here for eight days. Five times I've been taken out to be executed, and I was brought back each time. You should know that if your death sentence has not been confirmed by 'Szuch,' in other words, if your name isn't on the *Umsiedlung* list, they won't shoot you. My name isn't on the list so I've been sent back each time. Your name can't be there either because 'Szuch' doesn't even know that you're in the death cell. You'll be sent back from the execution, you'll see!"

By this time I was very annoyed. "That means we'll sit here in this shithouse until the Gestapo takes pity on us and puts our names on the list?"

"Calm down," said Heniek, gently putting his hand on mine. "We'll be sent to Block Four to join the group of Jewish artisans."

There was a sudden hubbub and we had to cut short our conversation. The door was flung open and a pack of Gypsies trooped into our cell. Some were very young, some well over seventy. There must have been about forty-five of them. Added to our ten Jews, we were now fifty-five people in the tiny cell.

There was no room to sit. We had to stand, pressed close to one another, the entire time from Saturday until Monday. If you can imagine how it feels to be in hell, this was the situation in cell 257 during these forty-eight hours. The Gypsies were talking and yelling without stop in their own language. I don't think they really grasped the danger they were in. We were drenched in our own sweat, unable to move about; the stench was unbearable, the heat intense. Water was not available. I remember going to sleep standing up; the feeling of weakness made me sway. I had only two things on my mind: getting something to drink and finding a spot to lie down. I did not even think of death, for this was worse than death.

Monday, at dawn, the Gypsies were taken out. I suppose they were transported to Auschwitz. Several days later it was our turn. We, the ten Jews, were led out to be executed. I was so weak that I could hardly drag my legs. Heniek, who walked close beside me along the prison corridors, strode with firm step, and kept reassuring me.

"You'll see, we'll be sent right back."

"I don't care any more. The sooner the better."

"Stop it, don't talk like that. There's always time to die."

The prison guard brought us to the office area. A group of women prisoners was waiting, facing the wall. Birkel and Alberts, the two Gestapo officers, stood nearby. A third, Wippenbeck, was strolling among the victims, whenever a woman dared to turn her head, he flogged her with his steel whip. During the beating Birkel would howl like an animal. His screams, mixed with the lamenting of the women, were enough to pierce the heavens.

The prison guard led us into the office and told us to stand to one side, facing the wall. We awaited our fate calmly.

The list of names was read aloud; whoever was mentioned took his place on the other side of the room. Heniek's name and mine were not called out. We remained where we were. Another Gestapo officer walked over to Birkel and asked, "What about these two?"

Birkel shrugged, as though saying he had no idea. But immediately he barked out an order, "Take them to Block Four!"

The prison guard told us to get going. As we set out, we heard a young girl sobbing. "I'm eighteen years old! I don't want to die!"

Wippenback roared at her, and the young girl fell silent. But her weeping voice rang in my ears all the way to Block Four. It lingered with me during all those months of suffering in prison. And even today, as I write these memoirs, I hear the voice of that young Jewish girl, a girl who yearned to live but was condemned to an untimely death.

Heniek and I were brought to Block Four, the block that housed the Jewish artisans. At that time only a few of them were at work; the others sat around waiting to be assigned a job. We joined the ranks of the "unemployed."

This "cell" was not like those in the prison basement. Actually, our quarters consisted of two large rooms with big, normal-sized windows, through which we had a view of the prison gate. Iron cots, covered with woolen blankets, stood all along the walls of both rooms; they were the first thing we saw. Can you imagine, real beds covered with woolen blankets! We had forgotten that such luxury still existed!

More than sixty Jewish prisoners were quartered in these two rooms. Half of them had work assignments. They went to work every morning and returned at night. That left about thirty people to welcome the new arrivals. Since Heniek and I were both in pretty bad shape from the ordeal we had been through in the death cell, we received tender care from our new comrades.

The artisan group had already formed a "communal aid society," under the leadership of two Jews: Gutman the bootmaker* and "Engineer" Hebdzynski. (Since we knew that this could not be his real name we had nicknamed him "Mr. Engineer.") The "Engineer" was very cordial and helpful. He showed us where to rest, gave us some bread and a double portion of soup for our first meal. Gradually we revived. We made ourselves "at home." From that time on Heniek and I were best friends: we were always together, sharing the difficult times and the few happy hours. We worked, ate and suffered together for eight months, until circumstances separated us. We were ready to lay down our lives for one another. Heniek was a courageous fighter, but he was also clever and prudent. At once a dreamer and an incurable optimist, he had an unwavering faith in life which could prove infectious at times.

"We have to find a good job, one that will pay well," he told me. "We must get our strength back. Only then can we look for a way to escape."

"You're a dreamer, Heniek! You can't get out of this place. Forget it! It can't be done!"

"You'll see," he insisted, almost quivering in his excitement. "We *will* get out of here alive. I've been convinced of it ever since the Germans nabbed me in

* See Chapter 11.

120

the ghetto. I managed to get out alive then, and I will again. Let me tell you what else happened there.

"By now I was on my own. I spent the nights creeping around the ruins looking for food and a way to get out of there. One night I found myself standing in a courtyard strewn with corpses. Suddenly I heard footsteps. When you're a hunted animal, nobody is your friend and everyone is an enemy. I heard these hobnailed boots approaching; I knew they had to be Nazis. There was no time to run. By now they were so close that I could hear every word they were saying. One of the Germans was trying to convince his companions that somebody had sneaked into the yard and was still there. I was positive he had seen me earlier and alerted the others. Trying not to make a sound, I dropped to the ground beside the two corpses. I lay there motionless. The Germans came into the yard, carrying flashlights. Carefully, they scrutinized the two dead men, pointing the lights directly in their eyes. They lit up my face several times; the sharp glare irritated my eyes, pierced through my eyelids; it took all my strength not to budge. I heard them talking to each other.

"'I could swear this one moved.'

"'You're imagining it. Can't you see he's dead?'

"The Germans moved on. I sneaked out of the yard, and leaped over the rubble into another ruined area. The ordeal of that night was over, but the memory lingers; even today I think about it: I was a hair's breadth away from death; if fate had willed it, the suspicious German could have pumped a bullet into me. Sure, I may have looked dead, but why take a chance? Bullets are cheap. Ever since that moment, I've been certain that I would survive."

I smiled scornfully, "Oh, Heniek, Heniek, you're a lucky man to be so optimistic." I said nothing more. I didn't want to undermine his faith.

One day a Gestapo officer walked in looking for a Jew fluent in German, to work in the prison bath house. I volunteered, and after being accepted, I asked whether there was room for another Jewish worker. That same day Heniek and I started our jobs in the bathhouse. It was a harrowing task: we were assigned the most difficult and the most filthy jobs. On the other hand we now had enough to eat. Every week we were given clean linen, and every day we got cigarettes as a "bonus." I smoked my cigarettes; Heniek hid his share; he gave them to the cooks, in exchange for fat, sugar and meat.

The four Poles who had worked in the bathhouse were sent off to concentration camps and were replaced by four Jews. Now we were a crew of six Jewish "bathmasters." We made ourselves as comfortable as possible, and became politically and socially active. Heniek did not participate in these activities; his chief interest was making deals. He bartered everything for food; as a result he was well-nourished and well-dressed.

He admonished me: "If you don't think about yourself, you'll perish. Don't you understand: we *must* get out of here. But you can't do it if you're weak from hunger and have nothing decent to wear. If you roam about Warsaw looking like a slob in those torn clothes, they'll nab you a second time. Do what I'm doing."

Heniek had hatched various plans for escape; I had to admit that every one of them had possibilities. We were eager to go along with him. We had the courage, but we lacked the means. Every plan we considered presented another kind of obstacle. And so we kept postponing our escape. Heniek, as the driving force behind these plans, automatically became the uncrowned leader of the bathhouse crew. And, as in every communal activity, when a project falls

through, the leader is held responsible. I always defended Heniek, claiming he had the best intentions,
that failure was no more his fault than it was ours. We
dare not lose hope. Escape from Pawiak was a for-
midable undertaking. If we failed this time, we would
succeed on the next try.

Thus we managed to endure until the end of
March 1944. By then, it had become evident that the
Germans were sliding rapidly downhill: defeat was
inevitable, and they knew it. Under great pressure,
they were more irritable than usual and we were
treated accordingly. We, the hundred thirty Jewish
workers in Pawiak, knew that when zero hour came
the Germans would annihilate us. We were worried
and frightened. Tension ran high, much as it had in
the final days of the Ghetto. The arguments and
debates followed the same pattern: who was more
indispensable, a bath attendant or a helper in a supply
room? Unfortunately, neither of these was a
craftsman, surely the Germans could very well do
without them. . . . But the auto mechanics and artisans of the prison workshops — that was something
else again. The Germans would be needing them
more than ever now and would take them along during their flight from Warsaw. These skilled workers
had the best chance of survival. . . . Our assumptions
were eventually proven correct. In the meantime all
the unskilled workers tried to exchange their jobs for
something more secure.

Heniek managed to get work as an auto mechanic.
He wasn't too keen on that job anymore: the bath
attendants were on the verge of carrying out their
escape plan and he didn't want to miss out on it. But
some of the other Jews had sniffed out what we had in
mind. Fearful that our escape would bring down re-
prisals on those Jews left behind, they did their best to
thwart us. When the Gestapo called for another auto

mechanic, the "Engineer," as clerk of the Jewish division, sent for Heniek. He had suspected all along that Heniek was the mastermind behind our plans and felt that we would be helpless without him.

Two months later we did escape, but by then Heniek was in another cell; much to our regret, we could not take him along.

Heniek did not die in Pawiak. He was one of about one hundred twenty Jews to regain their freedom on the site of the Gesia concentration camp. During the Warsaw Uprising of August 1944, Heniek, together with other Pawiak prisoners, joined the insurrectionists. He fought in the old city, then made his way through the sewers to the center of Warsaw. From there he and the other fighters went to Powisle. And there the curtain descended on the last act of the Warsaw Uprising.

Heniek was a brave and fearless fighter; he brought only honor to the Jewish people. He was not so much concerned with saving his own skin as he was obsessed with the desire to survive, to survive in order to take revenge on the Nazis for the massacre of so many Jews. "I must avenge the murder of my father, my wife and my child," he was always telling me.

Friends whom I met after the liberation told me about Heniek's bravery at Powisle. Then I knew that his dream had been fulfilled. One of those friends met Heniek in September of 1944, when the Polish revolt was on the verge of collapse. Heniek was suffering from serious abdominal wounds, and lay in the makeshift hospital on Gzerniakow. Then the hospital was evacuated and for a long time I had no further news of Heniek. Only much later did I learn that Heniek Lederman, my friend, did not recover from his wounds.

Chapter 11

Gutman the Bootmaker

Gutman the bootmaker was the typically refined, intellectual Jewish artisan found by the thousands in prewar Poland. He was thirty-five years old and had been working for twenty years. Although a highly skilled worker, his horizons were not limited to his trade. He was concerned about the world around him, had interest in politics and science.

In spite of his youth, Gutman was reputed to be one of the best bootmakers in his native town of Bydgoszcz. He always had more work than he could handle. He made such a good living that he was in a position to marry at a young age. Life was happy and productive.

No matter how busy he was in his shop, Gutman always found the time to participate in cultural affairs. He was an avid reader; Yiddish literature was especially dear to his heart. He organized literary readings, amateur theatricals and concerts of Yiddish music. Afflicted with a slight stammer, he was too shy to perform in public. But this minor defect did not matter.

Gutman was a likeable young man, of middle height, with sensitive features. He was always well-dressed. (The Jewish intellectuals in Pawiak made every effort to look like workers, hoping thus to protect themselves from the German practice of liquidating educated Jews. Our tattered clothing helped to maintain this fiction. The real craftsmen, those who could show tangible evidence of their productivity, had no such fears and made no changes in their apparel. Consequently, the genuine workers were decently clad, while the intellectuals wore shabby and tattered outfits.)

Gutman was one of the seven Jews rescued by the prison guards during the massacre in the spring of 1943.* When I was transferred to Block Four, those seven Jews occupied a separate cell in the same Block. Because their cell had more facilities and was more comfortable, we dubbed it "The Lords' Room" and its seven inmates the "Lords." Some time later the "Lords" were sent to an even better cell in the Women's Section.

Naturally, the "Lords" led a better life in prison than the others. As the oldest residents they were on very good terms with the prison guards, who helped them in many ways. And, since they really were excellent craftsmen their products in great demand by the Nazis — they were rewarded with food, cigarettes and other necessities.

Gutman was a particular favorite with the Nazis. A beautiful pair of shiny boots were considered a status symbol and Gutman provided them with the best. As foreman of the big workshops, his opinion and advice carried great weight with the Germans. Everyone, from the Ukrainian prison guards to the *Klawish* (Polish prison guards employed in the various housekeeping divisions), was forced to reckon with him. So it came about that Gutman, a Jew, was in charge of all those who were employed in the workshops: Polish prisoners as well as Jewish craftsmen.

Gutman never took advantage of his power. He had a strong sense of social awareness. He expressed himself to me in the following manner: "All of us here are abandoned and alone. Not one of our comrades

* See Chapter 2.

has a close friend or a relative anywhere in the world. We have all lost our kin, so we must live here together as one family. We must live not only for ourselves, but try to help each other as much as possible."

Gutman acted on this principle: he used his influence with the Gestapo men to benefit his fellow Jews. His main concern was in getting as many as possible out of the death cell. Frequently he conferred with Pietsch, the prison Kommandant, to whom he had access at all times. He would mention by name this or that Jewish inmate in the death cell, praising his skill as a shoemaker or tailor, adding that he, Gutman, needed him in the workshops. If he was successful, the Kommandant would release the prisoner from Cell 257 to join the craftsmen. But more often than not, Pietsch would give Gutman a tongue lashing for sticking his nose into prison affairs and tell him to go to hell. Gutman shrugged off this tirade. What hurt him was only that he had not been able to save a Jewish life. The next day he was back, pleading for another Jew.

The real trouble for *us* began whenever Gutman did succeed in getting a Jew out of the death cell: the man was brought to us, and assigned a job in the workshop. Then the truth came out — the man was neither tailor nor shoemaker, but just another "lipa" (a fake, in our slang) — and Gutman would have to cover for him. This could be a knotty problem — the hostile Polish guard employed in the workshops frequently betrayed the "lipa" to the Germans. Then Gutman would have to exert all his influence to keep the Jew on the job. More often than not, he was successful, but sometimes the unfortunate Jew was sent back to the death cell.

In all, Gutman saved about thirty Jews, most of them intellectuals, from death row; he strongly believed that this group of survivors, more than any other, must be salvaged. The thirty Jews owe their lives to Gutman. Perhaps their lives amounted to little here in Pawiak — still, they were alive.

In addition to Gutman's intercession with the prison Kommandant, he organized and assumed full responsibility for the communal work. When one of us fell ill and needed special care, it was Gutman who brought him everything he needed. During the summer of 1943, not all of us were working, and so we suffered great hunger. We waited impatiently for the evening hour when those of our comrades who were employed would return bringing with them pieces of bread, a little soup, (on occasion even a whole pot of soup!). The famished cell inmates hurled themselves on the food; it was the only time of day we could appease our hunger.

Gutman later enlarged the scope of his operation. The "Hotel Polski" Jews interned in "Serbia" had special privileges. As so-called "American citizens," they were allowed to hold on to their money and buy a few necessities through certain channels. Gutman utilized this trade to our advantage. I don't know where he found the money. In any event, from time to time the interned "American" Jews bought food for us, too. A major obstacle remained: how to get the provisions to us from *Serbia*, (the women's block). But, with the help of his friends the "Lords," Gutman overcame this hurdle, too.

If the winter of 1943-44 was exceptionally grim for the Polish civilian population it was even worse for the starving prisoners of Pawiak. The unbearable cold aggravated our misery because almost all of us were barefoot. Gutman found a way to solve this problem, too. With the permission of the workshop supervisor the Jewish shoemakers worked overtime to repair our shoes.

Gutman was concerned with the older, weaker comrades; and saw to it that they were assigned easy jobs. He brought them sugar, margarine and meat. Once he found an elderly Jew standing by the oven in the woodworking shop trying to stay warm. "Oh, my friend, what you need is something to warm your insides. If you had more to eat you wouldn't feel so cold."

The same day he brought the old man a package of food. He spoke to him kindly. "I'll try to help you in every way I can. Take this, and enjoy it in good health. Let's hope we live to see better days."

Yet some of our comrades resented Gutman's continual moralizing. The Polish prisoners engaged in the various prison "functions" carried on a lively barter trade with the cell inmates. A couple of cigarettes, a little extra food, could be exchanged for a suit, a pair of shoes or a shirt. Although strictly forbidden, these transactions continued to prosper; the Germans could do little to stop them. When they did catch a Pole red-handed, he would be taken off his job, locked up in solitary for two days and then returned to his old cell.

For a Jew to embark on this kind of commerce was more hazardous. For us, the road from solitary confinement led directly to execution. We tried to dissuade such "tradesmen"; they countered with fatalistic arguments: "What's the difference? Either we'll be shot or we'll die of hunger. We're not like the Poles — out to make a fortune. . . . But nobody has the right to stop us from getting a little piece of meat or a bit of fat."

But there was real danger for the rest of us in this disregard of prison regulations: an individual act of defiance could have serious repercussions. The threat in this instance came not so much from our German jailers, as from our Polish fellow inmates who saw in such trading an exploitation of their compatriots. An outbreak of anti-Semitism would be disastrous. Let the Poles rob each other, that's their affair, we figured. But we Jews must behave morally.

So went the arguments we used on our obstinate comrades. It so happened that only one person from our group — Ackerman, formerly an attorney in Warsaw — did pay the penalty. After he engaged in several such transactions with the Poles, the latter informed the German prison guard and Ackerman was put into the "dark" cell. Nobody saw him again.

After this incident Gutman could no longer contain his rage. One evening on our return from work, he burst into our cell and, in his broken speech, he lashed out at us. "It pays to risk your hide when you take from the Germans," he began, "at least you're making a conscious effort to harm the enemy. What's more, you can cool off a little because revenge is sweet. But to get yourself killed over nothing is just plain crazy. Listen to me and listen carefully." Here Gutman began to stammer badly. "I-i-it isn't w-w-worth it." The transactions stopped; not one of us got into trouble again.

Gutman had many so-called friends among the Gestapo men whom he had to engage in long, affable conversation. He often told us what moral anguish he had to endure to keep up his sham. One spring day in 1944 he recounted his conversation with Kloster-meier, the infamous executioner from ghetto days, "You remember him don't you? He hangs around in the women's section. He's nice and quiet now; but he used to escort the Gestapo automobiles from Szuch Avenue to the Pawiak, bringing terror into the hearts of the Ghetto Jews. When he and that fiend Wippen-beck rode through the ghetto, they would shoot every Jew they passed on the way. Those of you who were still there must remember how quickly the street emptied out whenever those automobiles passed through."

"That's true," echoed several voices.

"Today I rode into town with that same Klostermeier. On the way over to Gestapo headquarters on Szuch Avenue — the officers were having their feet measured for boots — he said to me: 'You know, Gutman, the war is coming to an end. The Polish workers of Pawiak will soon be set free.'"

"What about us?" I asked naively.

"Klostermeier was silent for a while, deep in thought. Then he changed the subject. 'Gutman, I know you're a real friend. What if I could guarantee that you will survive . . . on one condition?'

"'What's the condition?'"

"'That you help me out in an emergency.'"

"The conversation began to make me uneasy," continued Gutman, "so I began to question him."

"'Do you really think the war will be over soon?'"

"'Don't play the fool,' Klostermeier told me. 'Don't you know the Russians have reached the Polish frontier? The Führer misled us. He promised us victory and gave us a free hand in the occupied territories. Now he expects us to pay with our lives for everything that's happened here.'"

"Look at that coward," Gutman commented. "A beast who could slaughter thousands of Jews on a whim is now trembling for his miserable life. I couldn't stand it, so I spoke rather sharply:

"'That's no way for a German and a soldier to talk about the Führer.'

"I was afraid to say another word; I had said enough and I thought he would shoot me then and there. That would have been a senseless death, especially now, with the end so near. But Klostermeier was still deep in thought, and didn't say anything. When we reached our destination, he gestured with his hand:

"'*Alles Scheisse.*' 'It's all shit.'"

Klostermeier did not shoot Gutman. He continued to regard him as a friend. After Krupnik's escape,* he was very bitter; and poured out his heart to Gutman. "After all, they had a right to save their own lives. But to crap on the head of a German prison guard, young Rabke, that's what I call unethical and immoral."

It took all of Gutman's self-control not to laugh in the face of this Nazi now spouting ethics and morality.

* * *

One evening we held a reading of Yiddish literature, in which Gutman participated. Afterward he said to me, "You say you're a locksmith, but I can tell you're an intellectual. What would you consider your most important task, should you survive the war?"

"I would assemble and record data about German atrocities, to reveal them to the world."

"I agreed — that should be a major project. But I believe we should also keep a record of our experiences here in Pawiak. Start jotting things down today. You won't be able to send them out from this hellhole, but maybe they'll be useful to you, if . . ." and here he began to stammer, "i-i-f you get out alive . . ."

I replied, "Is any particular detail more important than another? We can't remember them all. But what *is* significant is the total picture, our whole wretched existence. It is so deeply engraved in our souls that we will never forget. We cannot forget. Whoever survives will himself be a living document of Jewish martyrdom."

"You are right," continued Gutman, "but I still believe that in addition to being, as you say, a document, each of us individually, must make every effort to take revenge on the enemy. I am convinced that I

* See Chapter 14.

will not die before I bury the enemy with my own hands."

After Gutman left, I spent a sleepless night, tossing and turning on my bunk which was situated high under the ceiling. I meditated on our conversation; that very day I began making notes, recording the more important events in Pawiak.

Gutman was indefatigable. He became deeply involved in plans for an uprising of the Pawiak prisoners, a revolt to be coordinated with an assault on the prison by the A.K. (Polish Home Army); the purpose of the so-called *Action Pawiak* was to liberate the fighters of the Polish underground. When that revolt did take place, I was no longer in prison and in 1946, when I was writing my book "Dark Nights in Pawiak," I still had no detailed information about the outcome. In later years, whe I did gain access to certain documents, I was able to reconstruct the entire event and the reasons for its failure.*

"Action Pawiak" did not occupy all Gutman's time and energy; he had his own plans for getting out of Pawiak. Gutman and his group decided to dig an underground passage from the cellars of the workshop building to the big network of sewers under the ghetto. The scheme was hazardous and presented many obstacles. The Germans were on watch at all times; the slightest blunder or accident would have ruined everything. Both digging up, and then disposing of the excess soil, had to be executed with great meticulousness. Vigilance was essential. They could not afford to arouse the suspicion of the Germans, or of those prisoners who were not part of the conspiracy. Despite these hazards, several comrades worked in the cellar two or three hours a day. By the time the revolt in Block Three broke out the passageway had been completed.

* Described in Chapter 24.

After the uprising was quelled, the situation of Gutman and his co-conspirators became even less tenable. The Nazis had found out that prisoners *could* revolt; they took immediate reprisal and shot forty-two so-called Jewish artisans who had had nothing to do with the revolt.

"Whose turn is next?" Gutman wondered. He did not wait for a miracle. "If you can, try to make a getaway through the cellar passageway now!" he cried out.

A group of Jews who happened to be near the cellar workshop began to jump into the hole. But the Germans soon realized that something was going on. They gave pursuit and discovered the passageway. Escape for the others was cut off.

About sixteen Jews managed to save themselves. Gutman was one of the lucky ones.

*　*　*

For several days they wandered about in the Warsaw sewers. They had no food, their clothing was in shreds, their shoes soaked through from the stinking mire. Often they were forced to crawl on all fours through the muck, because the sewer pipes were so low in some spots that they could not stand even bent over. They felt that death was near.

"Anything is better than dying in this filth," they told one another, and decided to climb out that very night.

When they emerged, the entire area around them was in flames; they heard the sound of gunfire. As far as the eye could see, Warsaw was blazing. They were in the heart of the city. When they found out that the Polish revolt had broken out, they danced with joy in the street. They forgot their harrowing ordeal in the sewers; they forgot about their hunger, their stinking, tattered clothes. They rushed to find firearms. German rifles and automatics lay scattered everywhere.

Whoever found a weapon ran to join the rebels.

Later I was told how Gutman, the stammering bootmaker, achieved his much desired revenge. Day and night he stood in the front row of the barricades, never pausing for a moment's rest, as gleeful as a child for every German he gunned down. Nor would he allow his comrades, the former Pawiak prisoners, to rest.

"Now you've got your chance to take revenge for the murder of our families, of our children! This is what we've all dreamed of!"

Gutman was killed at the beginning of August 1944, at the outset of the Warsaw uprising. He hurled a handful of grenades at a German tank: the tank exploded. Gutman died a hero's death in the conflagration.

Chapter 12

Who Was He?

"Give me a butt," I heard a youthful voice call out behind me.

I was putting the lid on the disinfection cauldron. I turned around and saw a boy of about eighteen: he was stark naked.

"How did you get here?" I asked. "If a German sees you through the window you're in for trouble."

"I'm not afraid," he waved his hand. "I just got back with the others from the interrogation, and I'm dying for a smoke. I ran out of the shower for a minute and stole in here. You have a nice face; I'm sure you'll give me a cigarette butt."

He talked like a child. I looked at him, and thought, "He *is* still a child. What is he doing here? And after an interrogation, too. Interesting."

By that time (spring of 1944), I knew all the ins and outs of prison procedure. I knew that it was dangerous for this boy to be standing around here with nothing on. The window looked out on the prison yard, where Gestapo officers and Ukrainian guards paraded back and forth all day. He mustn't be seen; above all he mustn't be seen talking to me. It was a great risk for both of us. After promising to get him a cigarette, I told him to return to the shower immediately.

As a rule, all prisoners returning from a Gestapo interrogation were taken straight to the bathhouse;

they washed themselves and had their clothing disinfected just as when they had first come to prison. The Germans were obsessed with disease and contamination, and the prison authorities were afraid they might have become contaminated with lice during their contacts with the "outside."

Thus, the bath attendants always knew what went on during the questioning, one of Pawiak's most grueling ordeals. Very few prisoners came out of it unharmed. Most suffered either bodily assault or had their spirits broken. We were the first fellow inmates in whom they could confide. They poured out their anguish to us, asked our opinion — did we think they answered this or that question correctly? Could their reply possibly be detrimental to them, God forbid; might not a careless response betray their friends? And so on. Of course, these conjectures were futile — the hearings were a thing of the past; nothing could be changed, and our advice had no significance. The best we could do was reassure them, encourage them, and most of all, just listen. This was just of the good deeds which the six Jewish bath attendants performed in the prison; even the Polish convicts were grateful and became very fond of us.

And now back to the boy. He did get back into the shower. A short time later I followed, looking around first to make sure no one was around. I wasn't afraid of our Ukrainian guard because he never spied on us. He only wanted us to think carefully before taking any action, to reason things out, to avoid trouble.

When I was sure there were no unwelcome visitors around, I gave each of the bathers a cigarette butt. I had to be thrifty, because I didn't have too many, and what I did have had to go around. The boy thanked me for his, told me I reminded him of one of his very close friends.

"What's your name?" I then asked.

"Schein."

"Schein?" I stared at him. "But that's a German name."

"I am German. I'm in the German cell in Block Three."

I began to regret our conversation. I didn't want to have anything to do with a German. The boy kept looking at me strangely, and somehow I couldn't tear myself away.

"Why were you arrested?" I asked.

"They wanted to squeeze some information out of me, but I'm not afraid of them. They don't even know how to conduct an interrogation."

I was astounded. This young scamp, who said he was a German, was talking about the Gestapo in a tone of contempt. What was going on?

The victims of the interrogation were being led out of the bathhouse. Schein waved goodbye to me and ran out. I remained for a moment, pondering, and then returned to my work.

The next day Schein was interrogated again. When he came into the bathhouse he walked right over to me, and told me, quietly:

"They don't believe that I was brought up in a church parish house in Yaroslav and that I lived there until the war broke out. The interrogator told me they had made inquiries in the church, and that no one there had ever heard of anyone called Schein. I replied that they had probably forgotten my name. I played the fool, told them if they took me there the priests would surely recognize me."

"What did the interrogator say to that?"

"What do you think he said?" he replied, with his peculiar contemptuous smile. "Will they go with me to Yaroslav? I was just making believe that I was sure of myself. Now they'll do some further poking around; but I'll have gained time. It'll be at least three months before they get an answer. And three months, ha-ha . . . that's a long time."

"Didn't they beat you?"

"I'm a German," he drawled, laughing gaily, as though saying: "I really fooled them, didn't I?"

All that day I thought about young Schein. There was something mysterious about him. He went to the hearing every day, and gave me a report each time. He had grown attached to me, as to a real friend. I must admit that I found him very likeable. One day he ran towards me the moment he came in the door.

"Today they tried to scare me. 'Dog!' the interrogator yelled, pointing his revolver at me. 'Where are your papers? I'll shoot you on the spot!' If you're yelling, I thought, it's a good sign. My story about Yaroslav really got them all mixed up. Now he thinks if he threatens me, I'll give him information. I made believe I was really scared of the revolver. I wept, asked him to take pity and not shoot me, because I was innocent and a devoted German. He put down the gun, but he kept shouting: 'Tell me where your papers are!' I kept crying, and told him I'd never had any papers. 'Before the war,' I said, 'I stayed with the priests. During the war the priests had no food for us, so the older children, including myself, ran away. I came to Warsaw, hung around the railroad station, and shined shoes.'

"The interrogator kept asking, '"Why were you hanging around the German troops? If you don't tell me the truth, I'll shoot!'

"'I was starving and I knew that our brave and kindhearted soldiers would not let a German child go hungry. And sure enough, they *did* give me food.'

"'You made three trips across the border of the Reich. How do you account for that?' His face was red with anger.

"'What border? There are no borders." I retorted

matter-of-factly, 'Everything belongs to the Fatherland, the glorious German Reich. We are rulers everywhere. All Europe belongs to us. For us Germans, there are no frontiers.'

"The interrogator was all shook up, and let me go. He'd had enough for one day. Tomorrow I'm going back."

"If you tell him you're a German," I asked Schein, "you've got to speak German with him. Do you?"

"Yes, I speak German."

Schein began to talk German with an excellent Berlin accent; I could have sworn he was a native of Berlin. He also spoke fluent Polish, with a Cracow drawl. . . . Listening to him, one was sure he was born in Ludwinow.

I interrupted his flow of German. "All right, I'm convinced that you know German. But since neither of us likes that language, let's speak Polish."

"Yes, but it's good to know everything," Schein enlightened me. "Let me tell you something else: the Gestapo is stupid. They caught me red-handed, but they can't get a thing out of me; they have no proof. They can't convict me of anything. They don't know the first thing about conducting an interrogation. If *I* were doing the questioning, I'd soon find out a lot more than they did."

"Schein, who are you really?" I asked quietly.

But Schein and his group were already on the way out of the bathhouse. Schein was questioned for the next few days, and we saw each other every day. One time the conversation turned to me. Schein wanted to know where I came from, and I told him truthfully that I had been born in Drohobycz, a town in Eastern Galicia.

"I know Drohobycz," he told me. "I also know Stryj and the whole region of the Drohobycz *oblast*."

The moment he said "Drohobycz Oblast" I shivered. He must be Russian, I thought. Who else but a

Russian would refer to the Drohobycz territory as the "oblast"? Now his background became clearer to me.

Soon Schein himself volunteered the information and told me what he had been doing in my native territory. "I was there in 1940 and 1941. At first I was in Stryj and then I was sent to Hungary to be a shepherd."

"Do you know Hungarian?" I interrupted.

"Yes, and Slovakian, too. In January 1941 I went to Przemysl, and since then I worked on the left side of the San River; I was in charge of espionage."

To test the truth of Schein's statements, I started to talk about the cities he had described, questioning him in detail about places and people only a native could know. Not only was Schein familiar with those places, he could even name the people he had worked with. Strangely enough, they were all NKVD* officials, men whose very names were feared in town.

Schein returned from his last interrogation beaming with satisfaction. "Today I pushed them against the wall. The interrogator used the same old trick, threatening to shoot me. Then he took out a camera. I knew right away what that meant — he was going to send my picture to the 'Dienststellen' (Gestapo offices). That really shook me up; it wasn't so long ago that they nabbed me in Dresden. I had all the 'goods' on me; it was only by some miracle that I got away but they've still got all the incriminating documents, including a photograph of me. So, I thought, if the Dresden Gestapo sees the picture they're taking, I'm cooked. My only solution was to play the fool. When the interrogator began to set up the camera, I made believe I didn't know what it was; I acted as though they were going to shoot me. I began crying and begging for mercy. The Germans just roared with laughter at my stupidity and pulled the camera trigger. In a paroxysm of terror, I twisted up my face so

* Russian security police, today called the K.G.B.

that my own mother wouldn't recognize me."

Demonstrating to me how he had grimaced, Schein distorted his features so grotesquely that I burst out laughing.

Schein was not called to any hearings again, but he also knew that there was no chance of going free. Although he was under suspicion, the Gestapo still possessed no clear evidence. Schein was glad that the investigation could drag out for months; there were signs that liberation was close at hand. He became a seasoned resident of Pawiak. Since he was registered as a German, life was more tolerable for him. He enjoyed certain benefits reserved only for members of the Herrenvolk, the super-race. According to Nazi doctrine even prisoners are divided into classes.

Schein was assigned a job as cook in the small kitchen which prepared food exclusively for the Germans and the Ukrainians. Because the cooks had to bathe every day, Schein and I continued to meet undisturbed.

He would bring me leftovers from the delicious dishes he served the Nazis.

Towards the end of May we were ready to make our escape. When the day came, I said goodbye to Schein. He was so moved that he burst into tears. Then he kissed me and said in rich Lithuanian Yiddish: "It's too bad I can't come with you. I could have helped you a lot on the other side. Anyway, I wish you the best of luck. I hope you will become free men! I'm sure we'll meet again somewhere."

The other cooks were already on the way out but Schein still held my hand clasped in his own. Then he ran out to catch up with them. I gazed after him, thinking, "Who is he, really?"

I never saw Schein again.

Chapter 13

A Share in the World to Come For Ten Cigarettes

He always searched out a corner in which to stand with the prayer book clasped tight in his hand. His eyes darting left and right, as though searching for something, he prayed. It was a puzzle to us how this little Jew, who bore the strange name of Kanarek [Polish for canary], had succeeded in hanging on to a prayer book in Pawiak. But Kanarek could do so many things which others could not, so we were not really that astonished. There was nothing particularly interesting about Kanarek. Nobody would have taken notice of him if he had not become an object of ridicule to the younger prisoners. Laughter and gaiety of any kind were rare and precious commodities in Pawiak, the usual mood was one of sadness and grief. Kanarek had not been singled out for teasing because of his piety. There were several dozen equally devout Jews among us; they commanded our respect. But half-witted Kanarek, with his religious fervor bordering on madness, was fair game . . . Conditions in prison are very much like those in the army: a shlimmazl quickly becomes the laughingstock of such a group and in Pawiak it was Kanarek.

Kanarek deeply resented the gibes and banter, and made desperate attempts to put an end to them. He tried to arouse the pity in the hearts of his tormentors with tales of his horrendous experiences. He spoke of

143

the suffering which he and his large family had endured on the way from their village in the Siedlce region to the Warsaw ghetto. After the liquidation of the ghetto, he had hidden out in a sewer, where he lay for weeks among twenty corpses, many of whom were his closest kin.

His tale left his listeners unmoved. Each of us had identical or similar stories to tell. In those days, if you were a Jew, pain and suffering were inevitable. The pranksters found out that Kanarek was a petty thief — he would take things even from a cell companion. After several such incidents Kanarek became the target of intense persecution, and the older prisoners had to take him under their protection.

* * *

I was able to win Kanarek's trust, as a result of a minor incident which occurred during Pesach 1944. Kanarek obstinately refused to eat chometz (leavened bread). He even stopped eating soup. In fact, he was on a hunger strike for the entire eight days of Passover. We tried to convince him that it was not a sin to eat chometz in such crucial times. During the ghetto-days the rabbis had decreed that it was permissible. The other orthodox Jews in prison had not stopped eating. But Kanarek the simpleton refused to yield. He must observe Pesach even in Pawiak.

"What do you want to eat?" I asked curiously.

"I want raw potatoes," he replied. "I saved up some fat, so I can cook the potatoes myself and mix them with the fat."

"What kind of fat do you have?" I wanted to find out, knowing it could only be lard. There was no other kind in Pawiak.

"What's the difference what kind of fat?" he insisted. "I just don't want to eat chometz."

I laughted, but Kanarek remained stubborn. Not

wanting him to starve, I brought him raw potatoes from the kitchen every day.

Kanarek liked me. "You have bought yourself a share in the world to come (Olam Haba). First of all because you're keeping me alive, and then because, thanks to you, this Jew can observe Pesach."

Then he made me an offer, which I found both astounding and comical. "Since you have bought yourself a share in the world to come," he suggested, "sell it to me. I'll give you ten cigarettes for it."

My first reaction was one of anger, but remembering with whom I was dealing, I began to laugh.

Kanarek did a good business with his "world to come." He didn't smoke, but he got cigarettes from somewhere and saved them to buy a share in the "world to come." The pranksters took advantage of Kanarek's obsession. Whoever wanted cigarettes went to Kanarek and sold him a share in the world to come. Kanarek was nonetheless a cautious tradesman. Before accepting the "goods," from a potential seller, he questioned him carefully about his mitzvahs (good deeds).

Kanarek did not live to see the hour of liberation. He was among the forty-two men executed by the Nazis on the eve of the Warsaw uprising. Let us hope his spirit is happy, rejoicing in the "world beyond" for which he paid to so many of his fellow prisoners in Pawiak.

Chapter 14

Krupnik, Where Are You?

From time to time a joyous event came along, interrupting the sadness of our dreary existence. During these rare moments, even the most confirmed pessimists could not refrain from laughing heartily. I want to describe one such incident.

Krupnik had been in prison for a year. As Pawiak's official locksmith and plumber he repaired the water installations, pipes, bathhouse, kitchen and laundry equipment. He was an excellent mechanic and highly respected by the Gestapo officers. Krupnik was a Jew, and as his assistant, he took on another Jew by the name of Domb. Domb called himself a locksmith, but that was stretching the definition.

The two men looked very much alike: both were the same height, both were round-shouldered and walked with wary steps through the prison yard; Master Krupnik took the lead with assistant Domb close behind, carrying the box of tools.

Krupnik possessed another outstanding virtue: he knew the Warsaw sewers like the palm of his hand (far better than most of the other residents of this, his native city). He would never get lost in the sewers. Moreover, very few prisoners, and certainly no Germans, were aware of Krupnik's expertise in this field. Our escape plan, finalized several months earlier, was entirely dependent upon Krupnik.

In his capacity as locksmith, Krupnik was to make

possible our escape at the final, decisive moment. The surest route was through an opening in the sewer; once inside the Germans could not pursue us. Since Krupnik was the only one who could find his way through the underground maze, our group of bath attendants maintained close contact with him. Krupnik, however, was constantly procrastinating. Because we were helpless without him, we had to be patient and give in to his whims. Our scheme of action was as follows: ten men were to escape through a second-floor window, cut the bars, and slide to the ground on a rope. We had managed somehow to get hold of the steel cutters and the rope. But Krupnik felt, and rightly so, that there were too many of us, that we were bound to fail. Since he was joining us, he wanted to minimize the risks: a smaller group, he reasoned, would not have to saw through the bars, and therefore guarantee the success of the scheme. Finally, the reasons for Krupnik's delaying tactics became clear.

Krupnik and Domb were clever men; they created an opportunity for escape which none of us could in his wildest dreams have imagined.

It was a Sunday afternoon in the middle of April 1944. We had set aside that night to make our escape. All the necessary equipment was hidden in the bathhouse. We would bring it to our cell in the evening, and make our getaway late that night. At about five o'clock in the afternoon Stasiek Kramarz* made a sudden appearance outside the window of the bathhouse. He was in on the scheme, and shouted to us, "Don't touch your equipment; leave it where it is for now. Krupnik and Domb are about to make a getaway!"

Then he quickly disappeared, not wanting to be caught talking to us. At first we didn't understand his

* Stasiek Kramarz, born Isiah Openheim, changed his name to Stanley Osinski and now lives in New York.

message. How could those two be running off on their own? They were supposed to go with us! A few minutes later everything became clear.

Rabke, the German prison guard, came into the bathhouse. He was nineteen years old, a Volksdeutsch from Pommern, more fluent in Polish than German. Rabke had been sent to "borrow" our rubber work boots — it seems that there was a flood somewhere and the men needed our gear in order to repair the leak. So that was the meaning of Stasiek's cryptic message! Somehow or other Krupnik and Domb had found a way to work in the sewer; they would make their escape that day.

Fifteen minutes later the two of them appeared in the courtyard. Both were in work clothes, and wearing our rubber boots. With slow measured steps they advanced, Krupnik, as usual, in front, with Domb several steps behind, carrying the tool box. Today he held, in addition, a kerosene lamp. They looked dejected and no wonder! After all, their Sabbath rest had been cruelly interrupted, and here they were being sent to do a filthy, disgusting job!

At about six o'clock, we left the bathhouse and returned to our cell, leaving the equipment in its hiding place. We knew that all hell would break loose tonight; there would be inspections of all the cells. If our equipment was found that would be the end of us.

The windows of our cell looked out on Wiezienna street. From behind the bars we saw Rabke, armed with an automatic weapon, marching around the sewer openings. He was beginning to show signs of agitation.

Bukowienko, the Ukrainian guard, approached him, asking, "Rabke, what are you doing here?"

"I'm keeping an eye on the locksmiths who went down to repair the well."

"What are you talking about? What well? Look inside and you'll see it's a sewer. When did they go down there?"

"It's been at least a half hour."

"Ha, ha!" laughed Bukowienko. "By this time they're near Marszalkovska Street. Rabke, you'll never see them again!"

"What should I do now?" Rabke was in despair.

"You'd better report it to the Squad Leader."

Rabke thought a moment. "I'll wait another half hour, and then I'll make my report."

Bukowienko's sympathies were with the prisoners rather than with the Germans. Knowing that within half an hour the refugees would be several hundred yards still farther away, he agreed. "That's a good idea. In the meantime, call them, maybe they'll come out."

For the next half hour Rabke continued to shout into the sewer, "Krupnik, where are you? Krupnik, you son of a bitch, come on out! It's almost time for roll call!"

But there was no answer. There was no sign of the plumbers; Rabke made his report to the Squad Leader. A terrible commotion ensued; a search party was organized — all in vain. Not even German "supermen" can find escapees in the Warsaw sewers.

After a while we pieced together the whole story. Krupnik and Domb had stuffed the toilet drains of the workshop with rags; the building was flooded. They were called in to repair the damage, but, naturally, they couldn't find the cause. Finally, Krupnik decided there must be something wrong with the sewer on Wiezienna Street. Technically, Krupnik's "diagnosis" didn't make sense; there was no connection between the outside sewer and the toilets in the building that housed the workshops. But since squad leader Hanish was no expert in plumbing he himself ordered the two Jews to go down into the sewer. He supplied them with rubber boots, a lamp, kerosene and matches. Thus equipped, the plumbers descended into the sewer and "forgot" to return.

The Germans did not know how to get out of this mess without compromising themselves. They reported to the Gestapo that the two Jewish plumbers who had gone to repair the sewers were drowned.

I met both "drowned" men the day after liberation in Warsaw. They were alive and well.

Chapter 15

*The Giant of Revenge**

I met Filar in August 1943 when I was working as an automobile mechanic and he as an electrician, in the Gestapo garages. There was a big difference between us, however; I knew nothing about automobile repair; he was a highly skilled specialist who had received first rate technical training. In appearance, he was slovenly and shabby; his face — haggard and unshaven — always wore an expression of despair and hopelessness. A pair of dark-rimmed spectacles jutted out over his crooked nose. His best friend, Frishman, was constantly scolding him for not shaving, or polishing his shoes, and in general, for neglecting his appearance. The Germans despised such sloppiness. Frishman was afraid that Filar's carelessness would cost him dearly. But Filar merely heard Frishman out, smiled and continued to behave as before.

One morning Frishman escaped from the garages on Dynasy Street. Filar refused to go along; he did not share Frishman's confidence. He waved his hand, and smiled. "What good is it, anyway?" he asked rhetorically.

* * *

* The information about the final chapter of Filar's life was brought to me by my Pawiak friend Stasiek Kramarz-Osinski. Kramarz-Osinski fought in the battles of Warsaw; after the capitulation of the Polish rebels, he swam the Vistula and came to me in Praga, which the German occupiers had already abandoned.

151

Months later, when the whole group of automobile mechanics were sent to Pawiak, Filar was confined to the cell next door to mine. I frequently observed him sitting on his bunk; a straw pallet makes a hard bed, especially when the straw is tightly packed and set on boards. But I doubt whether Filar, sitting on the pallet in the evening after a hard day's work, legs dangling, gave any thought to his discomfort. His mind was on other things.

Filar was tormented by gruesome memories. His father had been deported in the summer of 1942. He left the house one day and never returned. Filar ran to his friends in the ghetto police force. They looked at him as if he were a madman.

"What are you talking about? You want to save one old Jew, when even the young ones are being transported?"

Filar couldn't understand. It was his father they were talking about! What difference whether he was young or old? Whenever Filar thought about his father, he felt as though he were existing in a vacuum. He looked around with frightened eyes, and his lips trembled.

He felt still worse when he recalled a certain day in late June, a lovely, sunny day. Somewhere in the neighborhood of Okecie, Filar, his wife and small daughter and several other Jews were hiding out in a dark, tiny room. The short, stout woman who sold vegetables in the market had provided them with this refuge, calling it, in her genteel way, a bunker. Such a shelter cost a great deal of money. The family had been promised food as part of the bargain, but there were days they didn't even get a piece of bread for the child.

They had been confined to these lodgings for five months. On that day in June, there was a sudden, unusual commotion in the adjoining flat. A few moments later the door of their tiny hideout was flung open, and they found themselves staring into the barrel of a machine gun. A command rang out, in German, "Everyone out!"

Filar has only chaotic recollections of what happened afterward. They were all taken to Szuch Avenue and tortured for several days. The Gestapo wanted to know the hiding places of other Jews. At night Filar and his family sat in the "streetcar" of the Gestapo cellar. They were not even allowed to sit together. Filar was in one cell, and his wife and child in another, separated by a long corridor.

On the fourth day, when they were taken upstairs again to the Gestapo officers, Filar was confronted with Brand. He remembered him from the days when Brand used to speed through the streets of the Warsaw ghetto in an auto or a rickshaw, striking terror into the hearts of all Jews. Now, seeing Brand again, Filar began to tremble. "My life is over," flashed through his mind. And he was even more fearful for the life of his little girl. He could visualize the pale and petrified child clinging to her mother.

Brand was very cordial and affable. He asked Filar his trade. Filar replied that he was an electrical engineer. Smiling broadly, Brand gave him a cigarette, clapped him on the back and said, "Don't be frightened. You're not going to die."

The entire family was brought to Pawiak. Filar saw his wife and child being taken away, while he himself was locked up in the prison basement. In the long corridor, the Ukrainian guard relieved him of all his belongings. He even pulled off his coat and jacket before pushing him into a cell with the other Jewish prisoners.

Since that day Filar had not seen his family. Several days later he was moved from the death cell to Block Four, where the Jewish artisans were housed. From there he was sent to the camp on Gesia Street to join the group of Jewish auto mechanics. Mornings he went to work; nights he lay on the hard floor of the prison, besieged by millions of bedbugs. A few weeks later Filar and the other mechanics returned to Pawiak.

Filar was a first-rate mechanic. The work soothed his tortured soul and allayed his anxiety. It was only during work hours that his grief seemed to dissipate. But evenings brought back painful memories. Reliving the past, he suffered untold anguish. He knew that his wife and child were dead. In an eerie, cold-blooded way, he could pinpoint the exact moment of their death. He was sure that the assassin's bullets which put an end to the lives of his wife and child had been fired at the exact moment of his removal from the Pawiak cellar to Block Four. And yet, he could not quite accept the reality of this fact; the truth was too bitter, and he was too spiritually shaken and physically feeble to cope with it.

There were moments, however, when his spirit revived and he would be annoyed with himself for avoiding the truth. Ashamed of his weakness, he saw it merely as a form of highly-developed selfishness. In either case, we were his audience and frequently had to listen to his frantic outpourings of grief and despair.

"To think that I am still alive, and what's more, am clinging to life with all my might, while my wife and child have made the long, harrowing journey" — thus he would reproach himself.

Filar blamed himself for another reason, more concrete than the first. He had been a Zionist all his life; to be a Zionist meant that one should settle in Palestine and build the Jewish homeland with one's own hands. Several years before the war Filar had immigrated to Palestine and settled there. His father wrote him hundreds of angry letters from Warsaw, insisting that he return. He was growing old, could no loger run the factory by himself. He needed his son, couldn't get along without him. Now Filar cannot forgive himself for having given in to his father's demands. His return to Poland just prior to the outbreak of the war was a sure death sentence for his wife and unborn child.

Filar was strong-willed, but he had a tender soul. He was introspective, and he constantly searched his soul. At times he would tell himself that he was not to blame for what had happened, that he was paying now for the death of his loved ones by enduring pain and suffering in this murderous hole. At other times, he was not so sure. After all, could his torment begin to compare with the death throes of his innocent child? The question had no answer.

* * *

Now the German front collapsed outside Lublin. The Russian Army, in its race toward Warsaw, was pressing westward with overwhelming force. The Germans lost their heads; they knew they had to get out of Warsaw. So they carried out the final and bloodiest massacre of Pawiak prisoners. Unerringly, they selected for execution the forty from the group of Jewish workmen, and spared the true artisans, whom they still needed. They would be taken to Germany to work in the slave labor camps.

Filar was one of the hundred twenty Jews taken to the camp on Gesia Street to be herded into trains and sent to the west. The hundred twenty Jews were convinced that death was inevitable, and that only death could put an end to their suffering. Then, in one day, all that changed. On August 1, 1944 the Polish Uprising broke out in Warsaw. By evening, the Jews seated in the barracks could hear the sound of gunfire close by. Then a strange looking man appeared. He was dressed in half-military, half-civilian clothes, and carried an automatic. Pressing his face against the window pane, he peered into the barracks. Upon seeing the prisoners, he flung open the door and pointed to a structure on the opposite side of the prison yard.

"Run over there!" he shouted in Polish. And he disappeared. When the prisoners got to the building he had indicated they saw armed civilians standing outside.

"Who are you?" asked the Jews.

"Polish rebels. And you?"

"Jewish prisoners."

"Aha, Jews! Well, well."

The rebel leader ordered the Jews into a vast room. "Since you're Jews, and we don't know yet what to do with you, we'll keep you in here," he went on. Turning to one of the young insurrectionists, he added, "Better take their shoes, so they won't run away." Events were happening too fast. The Jews had just been freed, and here they were imprisoned again. It was bewildering. The world had been liberated from the Germans, and they were sitting here barefoot staring at each other. Then an idea occurred them, "Is anyone watching us?"

Several of them looked out of the window and reported, "Seems not. The rebels have moved on."

"Why do we need shoes to get out of here? We can get wherever we want in our bare feet, too!"

Filar sat on a bench in a corner of the huge room, absorbed in thought. One couldn't tell whether he was asleep, or unconscious. Too much had happened too quickly.

Someone shook him by the shoulder. Filar raised his eyes, stared through his spectacles, but he didn't recognize the man who was nudging him, and shouting.

"Filar, wake up. We're getting out of here!"

156

He got up slowly, shaking himself like a wet dog. "What about my shoes? I'm barefoot!"

"It doesn't matter. We'll go just as we are."

Filar trailed behind his comrades. Now his mind cleared. He recognized his closest friend. "Rysiek, where are we going?"

"Come on, you'll see. They're shooting Nazis and we have an account to settle with them."

"Oh yes," whispered Filar, "we have an account . . ."

Walking with his comrades, Filar was himself again.

His eyes flashed, his lower lip trembled. He was once more the Filar that we knew. He knew what had to be done. From the camp, the prisoners marched undetected to the site of the former ghetto. There they separated.

Filar and his five comrades set out for Wola. By the time they arrived the next day, they had found some shoes. The shooting had abated, but chaos still prevailed; terrified people were sneaking under the walls and running in various directions. The afternoon was beautiful and sunny. Rebel soldiers moved among the populace, trying to reassure them and restore order. Here and there, groups of insurrectionists gathered to receive new orders: the attack platoons were planning an action that night. German firearms lay scattered about the streets; abandoned tanks, seemingly in good working order, were in evidence.

"Boys!" Filar shouted. "Let's get to work!"

His comrades looked at him in astonishment. What work? But they soon realized what he meant. The six Jews, former auto mechanics in the Gestapo garages, set about repairing one of the tanks. Somewhere they had dug up the necessary tools. Filar supervised, just as he had in the Gestapo workshops; he tested, inspected and gave instructions. That night saw the birth of the first tank belonging to the Polish rebel army in Warsaw. The next day two more tanks were added. An official report was issued announcing the formation of the first rebel tank column with Filar as its commander, and the five Jews under him.

* * *

The dream of a memorable and triumphant Warsaw Uprising was short-lived. The revolt collapsed. Filar's group had been fighting on Czerniakow for the past ten days. After all their efforts, it was painful to have to abandon the big tanks; heartbroken, they had to make their escape through the sewers and cross the enemy lines of fire. All this time Filar grew in stature until he became a giant in the eyes of his comrades. He seemed never to sleep; he was always at his post, alert and ready, the first to respond to the alarm, the first to face the enemy.

Filar kept a constant, silent reckoning. He counted the number of Nazis he had killed with his own hands. He kept counting, but the total never seemed to satisfy him: his need for revenge kept growing. At the beginning he calculated one Nazi for every slain member of his family. Not enough, he reasoned. Consider, for example, his only child. Has the life of one Nazi the same value as such a precious creature?

Filar kept counting; the total grew and grew. But finally he waved his hand and just gave up counting.

One night a group of rebels planned to take over the house across the street which had been occupied by the Germans since the previous day. As usual, Sergeant Filar was the first to volunteer: he would lead the attack. The Nazis turned their searchlights onto the entire area in front of the building. But the rebels were adept at crawling over wet ground. It was the end of September; autumn was in the air. Filar crawled ahead, leading the way. From time to time he touched his belt, just to make sure his hand grenades were still there. He had another twenty steps to go . . .

now only ten . . . there they were. There in the ditch stood the sentry. Filar hurled the first grenade.

At the sound of the explosion, the rebels leaped out of their hiding place and made a dash across the brightly-lit courtyard. The grenade explosions, the shouting and the volleys from the automatics were all intermingled. The Nazis could not retreat; they defended themselves to the end. The battle lasted only a few minutes. After a while only intermittent gunfire could be heard. Then silence fell again; once more the illuminated area was shrouded in darkness.

Sergeant Filar reported to his commander, "Mission accomplished. Position recaptured. The enemy destroyed. One of our people wounded."

On still another night the Germans launched a strong attack. The "Tiger" tanks closed in on the very walls of the houses, where the insurgents had taken up position, covering them with a hail of fire. The rebels thrust back assault after assault. The onslaught grew closer and increasingly violent. One of these confrontations claimed the life of Sergeant Filar — first commander of the first rebel Panzer (tank) formation on Wola, Jewish ex-prisoner of Pawiak, auto mechanic of the Gestapo garage — avenging giant and heroic fighter.

After the liberation I visited Filar's grave; it was located on Czerniakow, in the courtyard of a ruined house near the huge Health and Welfare Department Building. It was not difficult to find — among the numerous graves, his was the only one decorated with the highest Polish military medal.

Part III

MEMORIES THAT LINGER

Chapter 16

Kol Nidre Under Loaded Guns

It is Yom Kippur eve September 1943. The survivors of the last Warsaw Jewish community have decided to assemble a minyan (quorum) for the Kol Nidre services. Last year there were still Jews in the ghetto; together they recited the Kol Nidre prayer. The next day they walked the road to death. We will do the same. Today we will pray together and tomorrow . . . who knows what tomorrow will bring? Providence will tell.

We were now interned in Block Four. The Jews filled up two vast halls. Being together made it easier to hold services. After everyone was back from work, we would begin the services. Atlasowicz, a former furniture manufacturer from Warsaw (now a carpenter in Pawiak), was to lead the prayers. We had no prayer shawls, but considering our situation, we felt justified in getting along without them. We managed to find a prayer book somewhere. Imagine, a prayer book here in Pawiak!

In short, services would be held. We were motivated less by piety or a need to pray, than by a burning desire to recapture the past. For a brief moment we hoped to establish a link with our previous life. That morning we went to work as we did every day. Until noontime, it was a day just like any other day. We worked hard, yet time dragged on. But right after the noon hour we sensed a dramatic change; the

163

atmosphere around us was fraught with tension. We didn't know what had happened. But then we noticed all the German and Ukrainian guards hovering around us armed with automatic weapons. (Usually they carried only revolvers.) In addition, each guard had a bunch of hand grenades at his belt. The agitation of the Nazis was obvious, their frantic running back and forth in the prison yard a clear indication that something had gone amiss.

Then the siren went off. The air-raid alarm had never sounded before so we were totally unprepared. Not once during my incarceration in Pawiak had Warsaw been attacked from the air. Would there really be an air raid now? In our hearts we all yearned for it. How we longed to see the bombs annihilate the Germans. It was our dream that such an attack would devastate Pawiak, level it; we were ready, even willing to pay with our lives for such a miracle. The air attack did not come, but the state of alert continued for several hours. Our exaltation turned to bewilderment and uneasiness. Was the prison going to be liquidated? In that case we the Jews would be the first casualties. In our state of mind, we always expected the worst.

All that day, the eve of Yom Kippur, we sat behind the locked doors of the bathhouse. Naturally, nobody came to shower. We sat idle waiting for the sirens to sound the all-clear. But the state of emergency continued. We were let out of the bathhouse a half hour later than usual.

When we got to our block, Kowalenko took over. He looked very peculiar with his automatic and his hand grenades. He prodded us forward with the butt of his gun, every jab leaving a dark bruise on our bodies. "Faster, you sons of bitches! Into the cell!" Once inside, we beheld an astonishing sight. In a cell in the Pawiak prison, ruled by barbarians bent on exterminating world Jewry, stood a group of Jews deep in prayer.

Atlasowicz was standing by the greenish-brown prison table which served as make-shift lectern. His broad back swayed reverently in a constant motion as he recited the ancient prayer. Atlasowicz intoned the psalm in a muffled voice, not quite his own.

"Light will shine on the righteous."

"And joy upon the upright of heart."

For a moment he was silent. Then he turned to the others, and in a hushed voice, as though talking to himself, he continued.

"Our Kol Nidre in this place is unique and symbolic. It is our continuation. Here we take up the golden tradition of sanctity handed down to us by generations of Jews before us. We are human beings and will not yield our souls to the barbarians; we defy our enemies by remaining true to our people and traditions. Therein lies the true meaning of our services here today. God will hear our prayers although I may not be the proper person to address Him in the name of this congregation. Some of you may not derive as much pleasure from my praying as you were accustomed to on these High Holy Days. . . ."

The prayers continued:

"May our Lord God forgive us our trespasses, for we are sorely tried in our suffering, as our innocent blood bears witness." The chant went on . . . "Kol Nidre . . . All personal vows we are likely to make; all personal promises and pledges we shall make. . . ."

When he came to the word *VOWS* Atlasowicz began to sob. His son, in prison with his father, was standing behind me. He too wept, repeating the same words over and over, "mother . . . mother . . . mother . . ."

Lame Mietek and I returned from the bathhouse together. He was a young boy, almost a child; he had had as yet no chance to develop. He did not know how to pray, had no knowledge of Hebrew. But he knew that he must cover his head. Since he had no hat, he wrapped a rag around his head. The melody of the Yom Kippur services awakened old memories; there was pain in his heart. How do I know that? Because he sobbed aloud and tears poured down his cheeks. He was not ashamed, and didn't care whether his companions saw his moment of weakness. Perhaps he remembered that he had spent the last Kol Nidre, just a year ago, with his mother. Mietek was a real hero. He had brought his mother to Warsaw from the distant East Galician town where they lived, had found her a hiding place. Soon after, they were discovered and denounced to the Nazis.

He is struggling here all alone, and the only memento of his mother is the tiny gold crucifix which he wears around his neck. His mother had worn this crucifix in Warsaw, hoping thereby to convince the authorities that she was a Gentile. At Gestapo headquarters, Mietek and his mother bade each other a final farewell; she hung the crucifix around his neck telling him: "May this protect you, my child. It's the last keepsake of your mother." Luckily Mietek was able to smuggly this double precious gold object into Pawiak. He never parted with it.

"Slach Na — In Your mercy forgive the sins of the people whom You liberated from Egypt. . . ."

After the evening prayer someone cried out, "Jews, say Kaddish!"

"Yisgadal Veyiskadash — Praised and sanctified be Your name!" The voices blended in an outcry of pain. Thus the last Jewish community in Warsaw, doomed to die tomorrow, paid tribute to those who had perished yesterday.

The state of alarm persisted through the night. Prison guards ran all over the prison, dogs barked incessantly. We couldn't sleep because of the tense atmosphere, the steamy air, our jangled nerves, and the thousands of images and memories racing through our minds. Only a year ago, our towns, although half-emptied, were still in existence. How well I recall that last Yom Kippur day. We bowed in reverence to the Holy Name, recited Neilah, the last Yom Kippur prayer. Quietly, the Jews shuffled out of the old synagogue. The bright silver moon gazed down upon the half-shattered Jewish homes. At that time those of our family who were still alive were all together. We thanked God that we were still breathing, trying to encourage ourselves with the merest spark of hope.

My friend David looked up boldly at the moon, as though challenging all the evil forces that seemed to have found sanctuary there. In a hushed voice, as though to himself, he said, "Next year at this time there will be nobody to come out of the synagogue. This place will be ruined and desolate."

I see him now before me, my friend David, the pessimist, the messenger and prophet of disaster, death and destruction. And now that time has come. The town is gone, and David is gone.

The exalted melody of the Yom Kippur chant haunts my memory. Whereas in the past it soothed and comforted us with its gentle holiness, today it reopens old wounds.

The next day, on Yom Kippur, we learned the true reason for the state of emergency existing in Pawiak. It seems that Polish Underground fighters had killed many Germans in Warsaw. Violent confrontations had taken place in several locations throughout the city. The Gestapo feared that the rebels would try to capture Pawiak, but the Polish Underground did not try to assault Pawiak on that Yom Kippur eve. Not then, or any other time.

Chapter 17

The Escape From The Boiler Room

It was the latter part of November 1943. By six in the evening it was already pitch dark. We had finished our day's work in the bathhouse and were on our way back to Block Four when we heard someone moaning:

"Jesus Maria! They're all gone!"

We looked at each other. "What's happened?"

The courtyard was swarming with people running back and forth. Kurt Novotny, with the Ukrainian guards in tow, came running up. Novotny, a former gendarme, was imprisoned by the Germans on various charges of criminal activity. In Pawiak he was accorded the status of privileged prisoner; in fact, he had more clout than the guards themselves. His treatment of the prisoners, particularly the Jewish inmates, was notorious for its cruelty.

The commotion was right under the windows of the boilerroom. We could see and hear everything. Inside the boilerroom, beneath a closed window, stood the Polish prison guard whom we had nicknamed "Felus." He was doubled over, his hands tied behind his back, weeping and moaning. Novotny was standing by the door, trying to force it open.

Seven prisoners had made a getaway from the boiler room about fifteen minutes earlier: six boiler room employees — the five Jews: Kaplan, Yass,

Zajaczkowski, Rosenblatt and Lach, and the Pole whom we knew as Heniek; the seventh fugitive was Dinner, a Jewish shoemaker employed in the smaller workshops.

Their escape plan was simple and had every chance of success. The back wall of the building which housed both the bath and boiler room bordered directly on Pawia Street. Over the boiler room there was a small attic whose outside walls were made of thick lumber boards. With a hammer one could easily pry loose one of these boards to create an escape hatch right onto Pawia Street. Since the attic was only six meters above the street, all that was needed was a rope on which to slide down to the ground. At this time of year it grew dark early so there was a good chance the prisoners could make their way undetected through the ghetto and then jump over a wall to freedom.

The workers in the boiler room were in an enviable position. They were the only ones in all of Pawiak with such an opportunity. The only problem was "Felus," the boiler room guard. The lads had given him a great deal of thought. In the basement under the boiler room was the hydraulic pump which supplied hot water to the whole prison. The boys decided to lure "Felus" into the basement and "detain" him there. The spot was so isolated that a prisoner could scream day and night and still nobody would hear him. The boys were in high spirits at the very thought of the trick they were going to play on the vicious and despised "Felus."

At five in the evening it began to grow dark. Stasiek Dinner asked Kudim, the Ukrainian prison guard, for permission to leave earlier; he said he felt sick and wanted to go to bed. Kudim was not a bad sort, and let Dinner go, but in doing so broke a cardinal prison rule: He failed to accompany Dinner to his block, to personally deliver him to the prison guard.

For this oversight he was punished later on. But it was a stroke of good luck for Dinner, for instead of returning to his block he went straight to the boiler room. Dinner's appearance there aroused no suspicion. Everyone knew he was a friend of Rosenblatt and Lach, and that he often visited them. Even "Felus" did not mind his frequent visits. For the boys in the boiler room, however, Dinner's appearance that night was the signal to begin the operation. . . . One of them ran out of the basement and reported to "Felus," "Sir, the hydraulic pump has stopped working."

"The pump? What a mess! What's happened?" shouted "Felus," irritated and somewhat frightened.

Furious, "Felus" ran down the steps to the basement, with two of the boys hard behind. When they got to the last step, they threw him to the ground and tied him up. True, the *Klavish*'s cries for help went unheard. But in their hurry the boys did not tie him up properly; they could have thrown him into the burning furnace, a fate he richly deserved. The entire expedition was to suffer the consequences of their carelessness.

In the meantime, the rest of the conspirators climbed up into the attic, taking with them an axe and a rope. In no time they had hacked an opening in the wall. One of the group then went down to the basement to announce that all was ready.

But it was not long before "Felus" had wrestled free of his bonds, climbed out of the cellar and sounded the alarm. Events moved swiftly from then on. The prison officials alerted the gendarmes (a platoon of men who constantly patrolled the ghetto site). It was only a matter of moments before they had positioned themselves around the ghetto wall. This was how matters stood; anxiously we reviewed the situation. The alarm had sounded at least ten minutes too early, ten precious minutes that could seal the fate of the seven boys.

In the meantime security inside the prison was tightened; we were locked in our cells earlier than usual. We sat in silence, sharing the same thoughts, praying for the boys' success. At seven o'clock the lights were put out. We lay wide awake on our bunks, alert to the slightest sound from outside. Our windows faced the prison gate, and nothing that happened there could escape our attention. Soon we heard the gate being opened, and an automobile driving up. A moment later we heard screaming and moaning. Someone was being flogged. Whips whistled, dogs barked, howled, and leaped about madly. Then another car arrived; the moans and screams increased in intensity.

By now we were sure that our comrades had been caught. We trembled with fear; we could not bring ourselves to look out of the window — from what we could hear we knew the fugitives were being tortured to death. But finally, one of us did glance out; he reported that Kurt Novotny, the German ex-gendarme prisoner, was conducting the beatings. Not one of us closed an eye that night. The savage flogging went on and on: twice prisoners from our block were called out to wash off the blood from the corridor floors and walls.

The next day we heard the whole terrible story. As it turned out, the endeavor was doomed to failure from the very start. While lowering himself from the attic to the ground, Rosenblatt had broken a leg. He could walk no farther, but he managed to drag himself to a nearby ruined building; there he slit open his veins with a razorblade. The Germans found his dead body the following day.

The other six headed for the ghetto wall as planned. The fugitives got to the wall, German police waiting for them. Lach and Yass were gunned down while trying to escape. The other four, Kaplan, Zajaczkowski, Dinner and the Pole Heniek, were brought back to Pawiak.

Kaplan received the most brutal beating. Both his eyes were gouged out; he died the next day. The others were confined to the dungeon, where they remained for fourteen days. Only then was the last act of this tragedy played out.

The Gestapo was not through with the three men; they sentenced them to death by hanging. The prison authorities printed up copies of the "verdict" and posted them in conspicuous spots around the prison yard. We were astounded. Millions of Jews had been slaughtered without an official "verdict," and here they were making a big to-do about a few Jewish fugitives.

The execution was carried out in a "festive" manner in the Pawiak yard. Two new Jewish slaves from the boiler room were selected to be the hangmen. The big cargo scale that stood near the prison gate served as the gallows — it was the proper height. The nooses were tied to the upper bar of the scale. A bench was placed underneath . . .

From afar I saw them leading out the victims. They were pale and exhausted and could barely walk, but they showed no sign of fear. Alberts and Wippenbeck were present. Alberts read the verdict. Wippenbeck ordered the two Jewish hangmen to place the nooses around the victims' necks. The men did not move. Wippenbeck threatened them with a steel whip, but Alberts stepped up. "Leave them alone," he ordered.

Wippenbeck turned pale and paused; he ran over to the gallows and quickly tightened the nooses himself. "Remove the bench!" he commanded the two Jewish hangmen. But still they did not move — as if he were not even talking to them.

Wippenbeck glared at them, murmured something, and then pushed away the bench. The victims remained hanging with their tongues protruding and their eyes rolled back in their heads. They died without having said a word. Wippenbeck turned to the two Jews, who were standing pale and agitated, still in the same spot. "Now you've seen what happens to those who try to escape from a German prison! That will be the fate of all those who disobey us. Now go to your comrades and tell them what you've seen here today."

For twenty-four hours the corpses were left hanging.

Chapter 18

Encounter with Dr. Emanuel Ringelblum*

The Spring days of 1944, before Passover, were warm and sunny, bringing hope even to those who had been living for years under the Nazi yoke. The easterly winds seemed harbingers of liberation and peace. Momentous news filtered through to us: the German collapse seemed imminent, our sufferings soon to end.

The balmy weather undoubtedly had a salutary effect on the population living in comparative freedom "outside." However, for those of us trapped inside Pawiak, the mild climate held little meaning. And what of the unfortunate people who became last-minute victims of the Nazis' frenzied roundup and execution machine?

There was no promise of deliverance for Dr. Emanuel Ringelblum,* his wife and son, all three new inmates of Pawiak. By morning of their second day in prison, we had already learned of Ringelblum's presence in the death cell. Ringelblum's name was known to all the inmates of Pawiak. He was admired by the intellectuals for his historical research and revered by everyone for his welfare work among the Jews in the Warsaw Ghetto.

* Dr. Emanuel Ringelblum, a well known historian, author and educator, was director of the Jewish Self-Help Committee in the Warsaw Ghetto. He initiated the first clandestine Documentary Center in Warsaw, concerning Nazi persecution of Jews. His invaluable archives were found after the liberation of Poland and are now assembled at "Yad Vashem" Holocaust Center in Jerusalem.

Although Pawiak was completely cut off from the outside world, some particulars of Ringelblum's misfortune had filtered in to us. We knew that Ringelblum, together with thirty-two other Jews, had been hidden in a bunker under a Polish gardener's house on Grojecka Street, that the gardener's mistress had revealed the hideout to the German police after a quarrel with her lover. It was even rumored that after the Jews were caught the gardener was hanged by the Germans right on the spot.

We were determined to save these new victims from death. But alas, what possibilities did we have left. Gutman was our only hope. He was to go to Kommandant Pietsch and beg him to assign Ringelblum to some kind of work. Gutman was more than willing. He had known and admired Ringelblum and was overcome with grief.

"We'll try to do something," he reassured us.

And indeed, Gutman began to search feverishly for an opportunity to get through to Pietsch. As for us, we resolved to send the new prisoner a message of solidarity despite the near impossibility of penetrating through the doors of the death cell. As disinfectant clerk, I could find, on occasion, plausible reasons, for entering different sections of the prison. But I was at a loss to invent even one good excuse for getting into tthe death cell. I was prepared to overcome all obstacles in order to convey to Ringelblum the message of the last Jewish community in Warsaw.

Somehow, that same evening, I finally managed to enter Ringelblum's cell. My stay there was very brief, but every moment of it remains engraved in my memory.

The cell was jammed with people, probably the same people with whom Ringelblum had been in hiding. He himself was sitting on a straw mattress close to the wall.

Those who had gone through this cell had left few mementos — only their names, scratched on the wall with their nails, attested to their brief sojourn in the death cell before the final journey.

On his lap Ringelblum was holding a handsome little boy, his son Uri. As soon as I got a little closer to him, I relayed the message of our group Ringelblum was greatly astonished to learn that there were still Jews in the Pawiak. When I told him of our plans to have him join us, he pointed his finger at Uri. "And what will happen to him?" he asked. "And what will happen to my wife who is in the women's section?"

What answer could I give him? We all knew well that even if we succeeded in getting Ringelblum out of there, by bringing him to us as a shoemaker or tailor, his family would still be doomed. I remained silent. "Then I prefer to die together with them."

He told me how he had been tortured by the Gestapo. The murderers wanted to extort from him the addresses of the persons with whom he was in contact on the "Aryan" side. They inquired about his recent activities. Ringelblum remained silent and did not reveal anything. For three days he was beaten. He showed me the black and blue bruises all over his body.

In the middle of our conversation he suddenly asked: "Is death hard to bear?" And then a little later, he went on with a voice broken from despair. "What is this boy guilty of?" Again, pointing his finger at his son, "It breaks my heart to think of him."

I stood helpless before Ringelblum. I did not know what to answer, a wave of sorrow swept over my heart.

I reported the conversation in its entirety to my companions. We decided to ignore Ringelblum's wish to face death with his family. Gutman promised to continue his efforts. He saw Kommandant Pietsch and tried to convince him that Ringelblum's past experience as a shoemaker would be invaluable to the workshop. Fortunately, Pietsch was in a good mood that day. He promised Gutman that Ringelblum would be assigned to work in the shop.

On the following day, while we were being led from our cells to the workshops, we learned that the Jews brought to Pawiak two days earlier were no longer in the death cell. They had been taken from the prison to the ruins of Zamenhof Street 19 and shot at dawn. Still, we kept hoping that Ringelblum would finally be brought to us. We were sure that the promise Gutman had extracted from the prison Kommandant would be kept. But Ringelblum did not come. That same afternoon, Kommandant Pietsch accidentally encountered Gutman in the courtyard of the prison. He stopped for a moment in front of Gutman and, with a contemptuous smile, said.

"You know, Gutman, it turned out that Ringelblum was not a shoemaker at all. But since I had promised you yesterday that I would let him go to work, he did go to work this morning."

With this Pietsch pointed in the direction of the ghetto. It was plain that Ringelblum had gone with his family and perished with the rest of the Jews.

Chapter 19

Recreation

In order to fully depict the life of Jewish prisoners in Pawiak, I must describe, at least in brief, the unique forms of entertainment which brightened our dreary lives. The precept that "one can grow accustomed to any kind of misery" was proven beyond any doubt in this bloody hell.

The average Jewish prisoner grew accustomed to his daily misery. He worked hard all day and learned to take for granted degradations and physical abuse. Resignation, in turn, led to a devil-may-care attitude, a certain recklessness. "Our lives aren't worth a damn anyway, so why take anything so seriously," sums up the mentality of the average prisoner in Pawiak. When he returned to his block, he could be with his friends; away from the direct supervision of the oppressors, he tried to escape reality for a few precious moments. Let no one accuse us of lightheartedness. Our few moments of recreation were dictated by the insecurity and never-ending state of terror in which we existed.

Some of the garage workers were able to borrow books from their Polish fellow workers and smuggle them into the prison. We enjoyed light novels and detective stories, but the most popular books were Urke Nachalnik's: these memoirs of a thief-turned-author, written while he was in prison, became best sellers between the two World Wars. In Pawiak, reading became a social rather than an individual recreation. A group of ten or more men would gather in the cramped cell to read and listen. One of the most gifted reciters was black-haired Rysiek, later to fight side by side with Filar and die a gallant death on the Czerniakov barricades; he never lacked an audience.

A group of older, dignified Jews, once members of the "social élite," enjoyed playing a game of cards. Since that was strictly forbidden in Pawiak, the players kept one eye out for the prison guards. Despite the risks, bridge and poker games went on almost every night.

These forms of recreation did not appeal to everyone equally; the "concerts." on the other hand, in which all our comrades took part, attracted a wide audience. Despite an early "lights out" policy, we used to arrange these concerts while we were still in Block Four. Lying on our bunks in the dark, we would run through the repertoire. Our "impresarios" were Michal Gaston, a young lawyer from Cracow (an amateur composer himself), and Wittels, a boy from Lwow, who had escaped to Warsaw from the concentration camp in Janow, only to end up like so many of us in this place, the victim of a denunciation. Gaston knew by heart all the hit songs that had once swept Poland; Wittels was musical and a bit of a poet as well. Their "concerts" were interwoven with stories and jokes, and stretched far into the night.

When we were transferred to the workshop building in the latter half of January 1944, we expanded these "concerts" into interesting cultural events. In our new quarters we were permitted to keep the lights on until nine o'clock. And later, when the second security shift came on, we were able to persuade our prison guard to let us keep the lights on still longer. We blacked out the windows, so the authorities would not find out about our activities. German and Ukrainian prison guards themselves often came to our concerts. They cramped our style a bit because the stories we laughed at the most were the so-called regime jokes. Finkelstein would get up and tell the joke:

"An old Polish peasant sat in a train cursing: 'It's all his fault, that *H*.' Because of him the war broke out, because of him my son is rotting in a concentration camp, because of him a bomb destroyed my house and all because of that *H*.'

"A young man sitting opposite the old peasant was listening. Suddenly he stood up, turned down the lapel of his jacket, disclosing his badge of office. He was a Gestapo agent. 'Whom are you talking about? Who is this *H*?' he asked the peasant.

I mean "Hoorhil" replied the old man.'"

In that case it's all right,' said the agent, mollified, and sat down again.

"The old peasant assumed a naïve expression:

"'Why, who did *you* think it was, Herr Gestapo?'"

We had hundreds of these jokes, but how could we tell them in front of a Gestapo official?

Some of our people worked in the prison depository* from where they smuggled out musical instruments: a fiddle, a guitar, and a Spanish banjo. Gaston played the fiddle; Wisnia, the tailor who worked in the auto repair shop, had a good singing voice and accompanied himself on the guitar and the banjo. He was as good as any professional. Their repertoire consisted of Yiddish folk songs, ghetto songs, old Russian and new Soviet tunes, and dance music. Several German and Ukrainian guards would always come to the concerts to listen to the songs. . . .

At the poetry readings, excerpts from Leivick's poem "The Wolf" created quite a stir. The book had

* All private belongings of the prisoners were confiscated and stored in the depository.

fallen into our hands by sheer chance. I do not consider this poem to be one of Leivick's best, but the subject matter — a rabbi, lone survivor of a catastrophe which destroys his entire community — reflected on our own situation. Moreover, our comrade Chill recited it with great feeling.

Another interesting number on the program was offered by Silberberg, our so-called mute. Silberberg was about thirty years old; he had an "Aryan" face but he gave himself away whenever he opened his mouth. While living on the "Aryan" side he had had to pretend he was a deaf-mute. He must have played his role well, because he remained there a long time. During our concerts he would enact a short scene inspired by his pre-Pawiak existence as a deaf-mute. He would show us how he had behaved in the street; another time he repeated his "conversation" with a barber, etc. The performances were always hilarious. And we never lacked for volunteers who were eager to recite or deliver a lecture; we even had our own magician.

Nor did we forget our Jewish heritage. The Okonovsky-Weissman* duet gave us Hebrew and Zionist songs. These songs were the most popular part of the program and brought the loudest applause. Sometimes the audience sang along, transforming the modest concert into a demonstration of nationalistic fervor. Thus did these enslaved human beings recapture old dreams, dreams which now would never be fulfilled. Had we been able to look into their souls, we would have seen that everyone had similar feelings of regret: "Why did I not link my destiny with the Jews in Eretz Israel who are even today rebuilding our nation? I would have been a free man."

* Okonovski, a former member of *Hashomer Hatzair* (Zionist Youth Organization). Weissman, a former Revisionist.

A member of the *Hashomer Hatzair* singing a duet alongside a Revisionist was at once a symbol and a promise of the ultimate unity of our Jewish nationalist forces. In those apocalyptic days, I could not imagine that there could exist a difference of opinion among the various Zionist factions. Today, I realize how naïve I was, how unreal our hopes.

We always ended the concerts with the "Hatikvah," the Jewish song of hope. The words may have sounded paradoxical to us — what hope was there for us? But in our innermost being, we felt that we were not the last generation of Jews. After we were gone would come other Jews; we sang for all those who would continue to forge the golden chain of Jewish life and endeavor. We sang with ringing voices, fervor and ecstasy.

Chapter 20

*Fragments of a Diary**

(*These are remnants of a diary which the author kept during his confinement. Most of the manuscript was lost during his escape.)

July 25, 1943

Death cell 258. Today old Yuzhviak was beaten over the head by a Polish orderly. The old man was really battered. I am so sorry for Yuzhviak. He's basically a decent human being. But our two brats, little Michalek, and Mardex, a child from the Ger Hassidic sect, keep on pestering and taunting the old man because he doesn't believe the Germans are capable of murder. "Herr Direktor," Michalek nags him, scoffing. "What do you think of the Germans now? Are they shooting people, or not? Maybe they are telling the Poles to beat up Jews, while they themselves pat us on the head? Some fine angels you've discovered!"

"What about the clothing we sort out in the warehouse?" added Mardex. "What do you think it comes from? Maybe you think the Germans send people to work naked?"

Yuzhviak groaned, and begged them, in his weary old-man's voice, "Leave me alone. I don't know."

Such a pity on old Yuzhviak. He would never hurt a fly.

* After the savage beating, Yuzhviak's faith in human kindness began to waver.

183

August 3, 1943

Night comes rapidly to our cell. Now the evening skies have a bluish tint, reminding us of the times when we still believed that they harbored our secret dreams and desires. The rapturous song of the woodland birds cannot be heard in our prison cell. What we do feel are the bites of the millions of fleas, they pounce on us the moment we lie down to sleep.

The nights are pitch black, even the moon is hiding from us. We are not allowed to light the lamps even for a moment. We must spread our filthy mattresses in the dark.

Kazik the *Starosta* says the fleas are a blessing in disguise; where there are fleas there are no lice. In other words, the fleas are here to protect us. Kazik tells us we should thank God for this blessing, but somehow we don't feel grateful.

We have discovered that one can grow accustomed even to fleas. At first they keep you from sleeping, but as a veteran of Pawiak you eventually forget about this plague. They bite, and you sleep on. But what about the new prisoner? By morning his snow-white shirt is completely covered with dark brown spots left by the pests.

Another scourge is the pail. The straw pallets cover the entire floor; there is not a millimeter of space between them. After midnight the wandering to the pail begins. You have to walk over your sleeping comrades, you trip over their bodies, you step on their heads and legs, and they wake up, cursing and yelling. Michalek and I share a straw mattress, right near the door and near the pail. Every night we are trampled on in the steady migration.

The older inmates can't tolerate young Michalek; they accuse him of being a spoiled, uneducated brat. All that is undoubtedly true, but it must be understood that Michalek was only thirteen years old when the war broke out. Then his father, Dr. Kahan, left the family during the exodus to Russia, and ever since Michalek has been his own boss. During the first years of war the little rascal had to provide for his mother. Then, in August 1942, she was taken away during the great "Action" in Warsaw. Michalek fled to the woods and lived there like an outlaw.

The older, dignified inmates would have liked Michalek to behave like a polite and respectful boy. Nevertheless, Michalek is a good lad, capable of being a devoted friend and comrade. One must know how to treat him and how to talk to him, something our older inmates are incapable of doing.

August 5, 1943

My assumptions about old Yuzhviak turned out to be correct.* The final blow came with the execution of the "Hotel Polski" Jews, a sight he witnessed with his own eyes. From that time on, he was no longer the same man. The aged face shriveled and turned yellow; the bright, vivacious eyes turned lackluster and clouded over with melancholy. He stopped eating altogether, he moved about as though crippled. Mostly though, he sat mute and motionless on his straw pallet for days on end.

Nobody picks on Yuzhviak anymore. Michalek and Mardex look upon him as though he were a stranger from another world. They are uncomfortable in his presence. Do they feel guilty? Do their youthful consciences bother them because of the way they mistreated him?

I cast frequent furtive glances at Yuzhviak. I know that the sensitive old man is experiencing a mental

---

* Our conjectures were subsequently confirmed when the Germans massacred forty-two Jewish "lipas" on the eve of the Warsaw uprising. Finkelstein was one of the victims.

breakdown. Any day now, Yuzhviak could die. I called Kazik the *Starosta* aside and told him. Kazik shook his head. "How can we help him?" was all he said. "After all, he'll be better off in the long run. I would give anything if I could die a normal death. You're right though. It does look as though Yuzhviak will breathe his last any day. He's lucky, really lucky. He'll die peacefully."

But now it has become apparent to all that Yuzhviak is in the throes of a mighty struggle. However, death cannot triumph over the spark of life still burning within him. By now we are sure that Yuzhviak will definitely not die a "natural" death.

At daybreak we were all awakened by Kazik's shouting. "Comrades, look: What is that?"

We got up quickly. Kazik was pointing toward the tiny window, from which hung a stiff figure, dressed in a black suit, facing the wall. Yuzhviak had made a noose out of his shoelaces and attached it to the window bar. At his feet was the wooden bench on which the wash basin used to stand. He had fastened the noose around his neck, taken one step off the bench, and freed himself of this world!

February 13, 1944

"The nights are growing dark," my friend Chill says to me. He is an attorney from Wilno, a writer and theatre critic. Here in Pawiak he has been assigned a "choice" job. He runs the hot water in the prison showers, and washes the dirty floors. The hope of escape keeps Chill alive. He is forever making plans; the plans may change but one condition remains a constant: the escape must take place during a moonless night. Chill has a ten-year-old boy in Warsaw whom some kind-hearted people are sheltering. Chill's heart languishes for his son; his one consuming desire is to see him at least once more.

The dark nights come and go, and still Chill's plans remain unrealized. He does not escape, and neither do his friends. Hours, nights and weeks go by in tense expectation, oppressing one's spirits, paralyzing the sense, draining away the last bit of strength, hope and self-confidence.

But nights can be an ordeal of horror and suffering. On one such night Yosl Kalinski dragged himself out of bed, looking to relieve himself. On his way to the pail he glanced out of the window at the ruins of Pawia Street. Yosl was struck by something strange amidst the habitual deathlike stillness: there was a bright light buring in one of the shattered buildings. Still half asleep, Yosl was unable to grasp the significance of what he had glimpsed. He woke up his comrades. "Hey, fellows, there's something going on out there. Get up and take a look."

We run to the window; an eerie sight meets our eyes. A big fire is burning in a crude iron hearth on the third floor of the gutted house. Something, or someone, is twirling around the fire. It looks like a wild witch's dance in progress. We rub the sleep from our eyes; the witches have turned into German gendarmes. Now we can make out a bareheaded man, dressed in the hated gray-green uniform. The flames spread a red glow over this uncanny mysterious ritual. Its glow lights first on one "dancer," then another, transforming each face in turn into a blood-red mass.

"You see?" says Yosl. "They've hanged the 'barehead.'"

"I can't see anything," says another.

"Take a good look."

"Yes, yes, it's him all right!" cries out the same voice.

We continue to stare at this unusual sight while the gendarmes cut down the body. One of them holds the

187

corpse's head, the other his feet; together they swing the corpse back and forth several times before tossing it into the fire.

The next day we heard the whole story: The Gestapo had hanged one of its own German generals the previous night. We looked at each other knowingly. After all, we had been eyewitnesses to the bizarre execution. If they're hanging generals now, then Hitler's empire must be crumbling.

March 29, 1944

The dark nights have returned. For several weeks everything has been ready for our escape, but we seem to have reached an impasse. We tell ourselves that there are too many obstacles to overcome. We can't always be sure of the guard on watchtower duty on any given night. Then there's Finkelstein — he has to be left behind. He's not a very sound sleeper and may hear us sneaking out of the cell. If he wakes up at the crucial moment and raises a rumpus, we are lost.

Each one of us knows that all these so-called hindrances are nothing but excuses. The truth is that what we are planning to do is extremely risky; the slightest slip may be fatal. The penalty in store for us would not be an ordinary death; they would hang us, but not before subjecting us to inhuman torture. How can we forget the boys from the boiler room, who paid a horrible price for their desire to live once more as free men?

Still, we cannot abandon our plans; we have made too many preparations to turn back now. Isrolik Hochberg, the locksmith, who goes to work every day in Gestapo HQ on Szucha Street, has brought us steel cutters with which to break through the window bars. These cutters, procured at great risk, now are hidden in the bathhouse. But there is no really safe hiding place in Pawiak. At any moment there can be a surprise search.

We also have in readiness a thick, sturdy rope painstakingly procured and assembled. It was Czechowicz the shoemaker who smuggled the necessary materials out of his workshop. The rope required about a hundred meters of the heavy braid used in making loops for officers' boots. We worked on it sporadically, snatching a few minutes here and there, but always in the greatest secrecy. The braiding process had to be repeated eight times until the rope was strong enough to support our weight for the twelve-meter descent from our cell. The rope is stiff as a board but it will work; we have faith in it. At present, though, it spells danger if discovered.

We know full well that procrastination is hazardous. But we lack the strength and courage to put our scheme into action. It is like taking a dose of bitter medicine. We know that ultimately we will carry out our escape plan; we will gulp down the bitter draught, for it is supposed to help us.

April 2, 1944

Bukowienko the Ukrainian is our friend. He looks like a Jew. He has a long nose, which has earned him the nickname of Yoshke. He is a fine human being, a rarity in this den of savages.

"Yoshke" thumbs his nose at his German superiors, Unterscharführers and Scharführers, all the big shots. He does not even carry out their orders. Several times already Yoshke was punished for his impudence. Once the squad leader even took away his revolver and threw "Yoshke" into the dungeon . . . another time Bukowienko came into the bath with a bloody face, and without his belt. He told us that Hanish, the squad commander, had slapped him around.

We try to convince Bukowienko that it doesn't pay to play with fire, especially if you have nothing to gain by it. The lame Mietek, Bukowienko's favorite, is constantly scolding him, "Mr. Prison Guard, sir, what do you need if for? You're being foolish; one day you'll suffer the consequences, and in the long run it will not do anyone any good."

"Ey Mietek, you son of a bitch," Bukowienko apologizes in his soft Russian. "You don't understand what it's all about. I can't stand those German bastards, so the words come out by themselves. What can I do?"

Pawiak can boast of very few Ukrainians like Bukowienko. He is probably the only one. His friend Barczenko, a guard in the bathhouse, is also a decent guy, but you can't compare the two. Bukowienko really is the driving force behind our escape plan. Barczenko knows about it, too, but he refuses to have anything to do with it. "Do everything you can to save yourselves," he told us. "But make sure that Bukowienko and I don't get into trouble. Anyway, I wash my hands of the whole business."

Bukowienko, on the other hand, doesn't give a damn about the consequences. He told us long ago he would help us, and now he is keeping his promise. His support is very important to us. He volunteered first to immobilize the Ukrainian watchtower-guard by getting him drunk just prior to our flight and then to keep an eye on him (to make sure he is sound asleep) while we lower ourselves from the window. This is not really a problem; a Ukrainian never refuses a drink. Bukowienko's help cuts the risk in half, and increases our chances of success.

April 4, 1944

Today, Bukowienko paid us a visit. Ostensibly he came to bathe, but Mietek thinks he wanted to discuss the details of our escape. Mietek says that Bukowienko is more excited about our escape plan than we are. Bukowienko tells us we must think through our action very carefully, use our heads. He is right. The best time to make our escape is between midnight and one A.M. Even if we manage to get out of range of the brightly lit area around the prison, even if we climb over the ghetto wall, it is imperative that we get as far away as possible from the ghetto itself that same night, and we have to do all this during the hours of darkness. At break of dawn we must find a hiding place in the nearest ruins and wait there until night falls. From all this it is clear that we must leave Pawiak no later than one A.M.

Now we have to decide on the best night. We left all those decisions to Bukowienko. First of all, it must be a night when Bukowienko's squad is on guard. But that is not all. Other conditions must be favorable too. The sentry in the watchtower overlooking our window must be an Ukrainian guard, one of those deserving of a horrible end (we know that after our escape the Germans are sure to punish him). Bukowienko is to give us the signal for departure on the afternoon of the chosen day. That will give us a chance to collect the tools we had hidden in the bathhouse. To make doubly sure, (sometimes orders for changing of the guard were altered at the last moment), he is also to look in on us in the evening. There will be no need for words — his presence will confirm that all is clear.

April 18, 1944

We must leave Finkelstein behind. It is painful for us, but we have no alternative. At the beginning we had drawn Finkelstein into our group, he joined us in discussions and participated in all the decisions. At that time he was willing to go with us; later he changed his mind, saying he doubted our ability to carry out the plan. He said we were good at talking, but when it came to taking action we would chicken out. I don't know what reason Finkelstein had to feel this way about us, but we suspect that, in reality, he doubted his own ability to withstand the dangers.

In any event, Finkelstein has bowed out. We've tried to convince him that we would help him every step of the way, lowering him from the window, and so on; he refuses to listen, he wants us to give up all this "foolishness"; if we persist, he threatens to disclose our secret to the others. We've just found out that the "Engineer," a man whom we looked upon as our uncrowned "elder," has learned of our plan. We have no proof that Finkelstein betrayed us. But we do know that we have to be wary of him.

Dark, threatening clouds hang over us. The engineer is carrying on a private investigation. He wants to stop us, because our success will endanger the other Jewish prisoners. The first thing he did was take away Heniek Lederman. Now we have only two choices. Either we give up the whole idea, in which case we must destroy all our equipment, or we take the greatest possible precautions to safeguard our secret, allow things to simmer down somewhat before proceeding as planned.

The first of the two choices is totally unacceptable. We are more farsighted than Finkelstein. We know full well, that at the slightest mishap we, the mock craftsmen, the "lipas," would be the first scapegoats. We are grimly determined to adopt the second alternative. Escape is our last and only chance, and we must take it.

But what is to be done with Finkelstein? He sleeps in our cell. How can we prevent him from hearing us when we get ready to leave?

Finkelstein is by nature excitable and stubborn. Should he catch us in the act, we could not convince him to join us.

We must find a solution for Finkelstein's nighttime

vigilance. Chill suggests that we give him a sleeping potion. Somewhere he has got hold of a few Luminal tablets, a harmless remedy. One pill is said to insure a good night's sleep. Chill slipped one of the pills into Finkelstein's coffee, as a test run. But Finkelstein said the coffee tasted medicinal and refused to drink it. Now we don't know what to do and we are in despair.

May 6, 1944

The nights are dark again, and Bukowienko says we should go. Tonight is the night! The red-headed prison guard has the midnight watch. He is despicable scoundrel. "A traitor to his people," says Bukowienko. Bukowienko is overjoyed that now he can teach the redhead a lesson. He has a big bottle of whiskey ready, he bought with his own money. We have no money and we can't pay him back.

Bukowienko reassures us with his usual smile: "You have nothing to worry about. Everything will go smoothly. Be brave and bold, and it'll all work out."

We don't share his optimism at all. We are facing an extremely hazardous venture, and besides, we have kept the problem of Finkelstein secret from Bukowienko.

Bukowienko tells us that he will appear outside our windows before evening roll call if conditions remain unchanged.

It is just before roll call. We look out the window. Bukowienko appears, walking slowly. He stands outside chatting calmly with the prison guard of our block. Then he strolls directly under out window and walks away. We have our signal. We will leave today.

Middle of the night. We are wide awake and on the laert. We prick up our ears at Finkelstein's slightest movement. Now he isn't snoring, he's turning over. No, we can't go today. We decide to postpone it. We try to sleep, and each of us feels as though a heavy burden has been lifted from him. It is really very difficult to decide to take the first step. We doze for about an hour. The door of our cell opens. It is completely dark. Mietek wakes up, but he can't see anyone.

He can only hear Bukowienko's voice whispering in his ear. "You sons of bitches," he fumes. "You're making a fool of me: Everything was ready, and you're here sleeping. You just missed a wonderful opportunity!"

"Mr. Prison Guard, sir," Mietek whispers back. "Finkelstein isn't asleep. It would be the end of us if we went today."

"Asleep, not asleep: You're cowards, that's what you are! Who knows if there will ever be another night like this? You'll have to wait a long time: The redhead is dead drunk, out like a light! What's all this hogwash about Finkelstein? You're afraid of him? You can't handle it? Don't you know what to do in a case like this? Either he goes with you, or you finish him off, and that's it:"

Not one of us is in a condition to decide whether Bukowienko is right, or not. We wanted to avoid bloodshed. We didn't want to have the life of a comrade on our conscience. We couldn't put to death an innocent man.

Bukowienko is furious. He walks out quietly, and we hold another consultation. It turns out that although Finkelstein isn't snoring, he *is* sleeping soundly. Bukowienko is absolutely right. We forfeited a golden opportunity. Still, we had no idea how deeply we would come to regret our foolish mistake.

May 7, 1944

Today we fell into Fruewirt's clutches. Fruewirt, the squad commandant is one of the prison guards and consequently the prime ruler of our existence. How can there be so much bestiality in a former waiter from Vienna. In the days before the war we enjoyed the charm of the Viennese coffee houses; we admired the refinement and politeness of its waiters, the kindness and gentleness of the Viennese people on the whole. But Fruewirt was just the opposite of all we had formerly seen and heard about Vienna. Everyone in Pawiak, prisoners and prison guards, Ukrainians and *"klavishes"* alike, were terrified of him. The Jews, as always, were the chief victims. Whenever a fit of madness seized him, we were the first on whom Fruewirt took out his frenzy.

Today, after roll call, when night descended dark and oppressive, Fruewirt came over to the workshop building. Our cells were on the third floor. He stood in the yard and roared. "All Jews out! You've got two minutes!"

He waited with his revolver poised, while we hurtled over one another in our haste, buttoning our trousers, tying our shoes as we ran. In no time we were all outside. Fruewirt stood calmly, a scornful smile on his swarthy face, the revolver in his hand gleaming by the light of the electric lamps which illuminate the prison yard.

We stood in two rows while Fruewirt counted us. Then he posted one of his Ukrainian assistants to keep an eye on us, while he went upstairs to search for hidden Jews. We stood and waited, wondering what fate had in store for us today. Had our last hour struck?

Fruewirt came down again. He hadn't found anyone, and this seemed to pacify him. Nevertheless, he ordered us to march forward, into the middle of the yard, and then issued a series of orders. He kept us busy for two hours performing the most strenuous gymnastics. We ran very fast, then we crawled on all fours. When we were so spent that we could no longer stand on our feet, Fruewirt told us we had a "job" to do. Big cartons of tin cans, and bags of chemicals were piled up in the yard. The Germans had confiscated this material a week ago from a munitions and explosives factory operated by the Polish Underground Army. There were several tons of the stuff lying around the Pawiak yard. Fruewirt ordered us to carry the backbreaking loads from one side of the yard to the other. He kept us there until daybreak.

All that long night, Chill was by my side. "You see," he whispered. "The nights are dark and our situation is growing worse. I feel that the end is near. We mustn't delay, because soon it'll be too late."

Chill was right. I knew that.

Chapter 21

The Escape

May 30, 1944

We must go today. Today or never. Fruewirt's persecution is becoming intolerable. He is on guard duty every other day; he torments and harasses us with ever growing fury, as though he sensed that his own end was near. He takes revenge on us for the humiliating defeats which the Germans are suffering on the battlefront. He consoles himself with our anguish. But we are no longer able to bear this torment. We must put an end to it. Yes, we must go today, at all costs.

Bukowienko was angry at us because of the other night, but we were able to appease him. He told us he would try again. He will give us one more chance, and won't let us make a fool of him again. Once again he had to buy whiskey and rolls and sausages; again it cost him a thousand zlotys. Will we ever be able to repay him?

The procedure hasn't changed. Bukowienko made his appearance under our window, before evening roll call to indicate the "all clear."

The lame Mietek is the driving force behind the whole operation. He has decided that the operation must get underway now, before roll call. The workshops are empty at that time and it is easy for Mietek to get in with his duplicate keys. Now he and the "mute" Silberberg are there with the big steel cutters. In a moment the two bars on the window are snipped apart. The whole maneuver took five minutes, and they are back with us unobserved.

Now we are all assembled at roll call. On the surface we seem placid, as always, but each one of us is tense and shaken. If we don't escape today, the cut bars will be discovered tomorrow.

After roll call we return to our cell, acting as though nothing were happening. We get undressed, stretch out on our bunks, and make believe we are asleep. In the dark, we can hear Finkelstein snoring from the bottom bunk. That's our signal! We get dressed without making a sound. We lie down again and wait.

It is essential for us to know the time. That's not an easy affair in Pawiak — prisoners are forbidden to have timepieces. But Mietek has managed to sneak a wristwatch from somewhere. It is not very accurate, but it gives us an idea of the time. Mietek is the youngest of our group, but the most efficient, and capable. He has taken command. At midnight, he gives the signal. One by one we slip off our bunks. Barefoot, carrying our shoes, we make our way from the third floor down to the second, where the workshops are. Mietek leads the way, unlocking all the doors. When we have passed through, he locks them behind us.

Four of us have left the cell: Mietek, Chill, Dattyner and I, all bath attendants. Finkelstein stayed behind of course and Heniek Lederman was no longer with us. He was working in the garages as an auto mechanic.

I remember clearly the moment when we took our first step toward freedom. I observed my companions objectively, even dispassionately. Chill looked the oddest; in an effort to disguise his Jewish appearance, he was wearing a funny-looking hat but he succeeded merely in looking like a Gypsy. His face, gaunt and unusually pale, stood out in the darkness. His lips twitched nervously, and I could hear his teeth chattering. The other two men were more in control. Mietek was a little nervous too, but kept his head and made a firm commander. I can't say anything about my own behavior, but later Mietek praised me for my coolness at the critical moment.

The six men who would make the break together with us were already waiting in the big room where the workshops were located. They were: Gurman the tailor; Lifshitz, the orderly, Czechowicz and Zarembski, shoemakers; the "mute" Silberberg; and Jakubowicz, the workshop orderly who had given Mietek the keys to the doors.

There isn't a moment to lose. Mietek and I take hold of the pre-cut iron window bars and pry them forcibly apart. Now the opening is big enough for a man to pass through. We fasten the rope and drop it out of the window, making sure it reaches the ground. Leaning out of the window we check, and double check. Yes, it reaches the ground. We have no trouble verifying that since the area is brightly lit by numerous spotlights. Only now does the full extent of our danger hit us in the face. *We* have a clear view of everything going on in the street below us. Conversely, the sentry can spot *us* at any moment. Of what use to us now are Chill's "dark nights"? Only a miracle could save us now: we go ahead.

"Mute" Silberberg is the first to vanish into the floodlighted abyss. As he lowers himself, his shoes clank loudly and resoundingly. We listen and wait with bated breath. Now Silberberg reaches the ground. Silence. No shots yet. The second man follows, then the third and the others.

I am the seventh. I get up on the window, seize the rope firmly, push myself through the opening. For a moment I am suspended over the abyss. Then I begin to lower myself. The rope is stiff and hard; it cuts into my palms, tearing away chunks of skin and flesh. But I hold on. It takes no more than two seconds and I feel the ground under my feet. All is quiet. Now I am at the corner of Wiezienna and Pawia Streets, where the others are waiting. The last three join us, and we set out together. The route has been planned before — a short distance along Pawia Street, then Zamenhof Street until we reach Przejazd and the ghetto wall (somewhat lower here than elsewhere). A jump over the wall and we are on the "Aryan" side. But we're not out of danger yet. Far from it.

But for now we must take off our shoes and continue on our way barefoot. This has a double advantage: we can hear anyone but nobody can hear us. If a German police patrol appears, we will hear the clank of their heavy boots long before they can see us.

We stride unnoticed along the deserted streets of Warsaw, trying to get as far as possible away from the ghetto walls. We know that is the most likely area for tomorrow's search. We keep walking at a fast pace, almost running; suddenly we hear the shrill sound of a whistle. We turn and run in an opposite direction. There are two bodies lying on the ground: a quick glance tells us they are two Polish night watchmen. Apparently *they* saw us, got frightened and are now pretending to be asleep. We change directions again; at daybreak we reach Mirowskie Hale.* We make a dash to Grzybowska Street where there are many demolished houses, grim reminders of the bombings of 1939. We find the largest of these ruins and crawl into a deep hole. Totally exhausted, but at least we have a place to rest. We will remain here all day, because today the search for us will be the most widespread.

* A big market place

200

Only now do I become aware of the sharp stinging pain in my palms. But that is of minor importance in view of our present situation. For the time being we are safe, and that is all that matters.

The optimism that buoyed us while we were hiding out in the ruins on Grzybowska Street turns out to be premature. At that moment we had no way of knowing that the worst of our ordeal would begin tomorrow, after we had left the devastated site.

Chapter 22

Road to Freedom

We chose the late afternoon for our getaway from the ruins. At that hour of the day the trolleys would be crowded, people would be milling through the streets on their way home. Our little band of refugees split up: Mietek, Chill and I went off together. Our road led to Saska Kepa, a part of town with lovely garden homes, bordering the right bank of the Vistula and south of Praga.

When we got off the trolley on Francuska Street, the early summer sun was about to set. Throngs of well-dressed young people were strolling leisurely along the street. It was a typical early summer evening in one of Warsaw's better neighborhoods. I admired the flower gardens, spreading their warm colors alongside the tastefully constructed houses. At the same time I was troubled somewhat by the odd thought that I was back on the "Aryan" side and must now resume the mask; I dare not abandon it, ever.

Actually, Chill hoped to run into some old acquaintances among the strollers. We had nowhere to turn on our first night of freedom; perhaps a friend could offer us temporary shelter. Chill's friends were mostly theatre people — actors, playwrights and directors. He knew where most of them lived, but was careful not to make unannounced visits which could result in complications for both parties. Meanwhile the curfew hour was approaching; with every minute the problem of securing a roof over our head became more urgent.

Chill also knew a janitor living on Berezynska Street. He was a deeply religious man, a member of the Baptist sect. But Chill said we should rely on him in an emergency only. There was a good reason for Chill's hesitation; opposite the janitor's house lived the woman who was sheltering Lolek, Chill's ten-year-old son; too close a proximity to his son might be dangerous for them both. I had no choice but to stick with my two friends. My brother was gone; I had no other acquaintances or connection.

* * *

The loss of my brother was an immeasurably tragic and bitter event. He died in Pawiak; I was almost an eye-witness to his death. It was on a fall day in November 1943. I was standing at the window of the bathhouse, looking out onto the prisonyard. I did not often stand at that window as I hated the reality of the prison and did not want to be a witness to events in the yard.

This time, however, some inner force pushed me to the window. A group of prisoners whom the Nazis had just brought from the city was being taken out of the prison office and led to the main prison building. Suddenly, I began trembling all over. I tottered and fell to my knees. Heniek Lederman, who stood not far away, ran up to me, "What's wrong?" he asked anxiously.

I stretched out my hand in the direction of the procession of prisoners. "Look, they've caught my brother. He's right there in the front row." He was dressed in his old navy blue overcoat. His hat was in his hand and his bare head, which only a short time back was covered with a thick, dark forelock, was now white.

A moment later the whole group entered the

prison building. I stood frozen by the window, not knowing what to do with myself; how could I save from death the last remaining member of my family.

"Maybe you ought to talk to Gutman," Heniek suggested. I had given Gutman some thought myself. Now I ran over to the shoemaker and begged him to help me. Perhaps he could exert his influence, have my brother brought into our work group. I also asked Wanat, the prison administration clerk, in what cell my brother had been locked up. If only it was #258, I prayed silently, I'd have more time to do something for him. But Wanat knew that my brother was a "plus" in cell 257. Gutman could do nothing. My brother was added to the ever growing number of Jews who died a martyr's death, "Al Kiddush Hashem."

* * *

The curfew hour was already upon us. In the end we were forced to spend the night with the janitor on Berezynska Street. In the cellar was a dingy laundry room. It looked as if it had not served its original purpose in years. On the stone floor lay several sacks of straw. It was apparent that others, like us, had found a night's lodging here.

The janitor was a poor man. He and his two children often suffered from hunger. We knew that we could expect no help with regard to food from him. Luckily, we had brought a little money with us from prison, enough to get us through the first day.

Both my injured palms now began to ache very painfully. The wound on my right hand had already begun to swell considerably. With a muffled groan, I slumped down on the filthy bed. Mietek came up to me, "Hold on; I'll get you something."

He managed to find a drug store just before curfew and buy the necessary medication. With the remaining money he bought a small loaf of bread and a piece of salami to still our hunger.

The following morning both Mietek and I set out for the very center of Warsaw, to an address we had received from a friendly Polish prisoner in Block Three. Chill wanted to stay where he was. Without the two of us, he felt, it would be easy for him to settle down here.

We came to a store dealing in second-hand merchandise — its underground business was quite different. We reported, giving the proprietor all the proper passwords that we had previously rehearsed with our Pawiak friend. The owner questioned us about life in prison; he was eager for news of his friends held captive there. We knew some of them and could tell him about their current state and tribulations. Finally he asked, "What do you need?"

We asked three things of him: documents, a little money and, most important, a place to live in safety. We stayed on the premises overnight, locked in securely by the owner. The next morning he came back, accompanied by two wizened old women dressed in long black clothes, with shawls on their heads. The ladies took us to Chmielna Street and installed us in the janitor's cramped quarters.

I can still see the two beds, piled high with cushions and quilts and the small window looking out on the narrow yard. Above the flower-bedecked altar stood the figure of the Holy Mother with the Child Jesus. The neighbors, women for the most part, would gather every evening and conduct services at this altar.

Our old ladies told us to behave with great circumspection; the neighbors must not suspect our presence in the building. On that very same day a young man from the Organization came to see us. He took photographs, promising to be back in a few days with the completed documents. Meanwhile we were to remain here; the two old women would bring us food every day.

A week later we received our papers and a small amount of cash. The most essential, a roof over our heads, could not be arranged by the Organization. We were told to leave this place. We were to walk in the direction of Siedlce and there seek out the partisans. We were not given a recommendation to any particular group, so the trip to Siedlce turned out to be a total waste. Everyone must have sensed that we were Jews.

With our new documents and the little help we had received from the Organization, we returned to Saska Kepa. There we found Chill, in the same state in which we had left him. All his acquaintances had simply vanished. He was still spending his nights in the janitor's cellar and wandering about the streets and parks by day.

Such a mode of living entailed great danger for all of us. But for the moment we had no choice. We decided to stick together and find an alternative to our nomadic existence. Just how precarious our situation was, we were to discover a few days later.

We had just returned from our daily walk when we heard the echo of heavy steps outside our cellar hideout. Three Polish policemen, dressed in their dark blue uniforms, stood in the doorway. They pointed their guns at us and ordered us outdoors. Then they led us into the janitor's house and told us to lie down on the ground, a technique these collaborators had learned from their Gestapo mentors. Mietek did not lose his head. He sensed that we could buy ourselves out of this jam. While lying on the floor he began a conversation with the more humane-looking of the three cops. This man told Mietek that they had been summoned here on some "misunderstanding," something to do with stolen chickens. An aggrieved neighbor had somehow gotten the idea in her head that the hens had been stolen by the three "strangers" who had recently been seen in the Baptist janitor's house. The neighbor reported to the police who had now come to "have a look" at us.

"I don't want to have a hand in your death," the first policeman told Mietek, "especially now when the fall of the Germans is imminent. But, that one," pointing to the tall policeman, "is an especially vicious man. You'll have to give him something."

All Mietek had left in his possession was a five hundred zloty bill. He gave it to the "friendly" policeman, who brought it over to his tall colleague; the two men exchanged a few words before he came back to Mietek. "OK for now, but you'll have to make it more," he warned.

"I'll have it by next week," Mietek assured him.

"So next week you'll bring another five hundred. Go to the commissariat and ask for Waclaw."

It was already dark outside when they took us out of the house. They cautioned us not to spend the night here, but instead to find a spot inside one of the ruined buildings nearby.

* * *

Ultimately we had to return to our janitor's cellar because we couldn't find a place to sleep. During the day we dragged ourselves through the streets. I felt as though there was a noose around my neck that was drawing tighter and tighter. I said to my two friends, "We don't have to make our enemies' job any easier. Let's remember that we dare not show ourselves in the street together. Should they, God forbid, catch one of us, let the other two remain free. If we continue being seen together, they could take all three of us in one fell swoop."

The next morning we went on our separate walks and it wasn't until evening that we met again in our cellar. We were wary about our neighbors, keeping out of sight as much as possible. But circumspection and prudence did not come naturally to Mietek; he even began an affair with our janitor's daughter! They went about everywhere together, oblivious to the danger. I was always careful and kept to myself during the day. No doubt that was one of the reasons I survived that frightful period.

For some time now the Warsaw Nazi newspaper had been writing articles about "shortening" of the German lines and "regrouping" the Wehrmacht positions. All these "miracles," according to the paper, were taking place near cities on Polish territory. It was clear that the German withdrawal was now proceeding at full speed on all fronts and, in great measure, on Polish soil as well. In a very short time the Russian Army would reach Warsaw. Then one day came the report of the unsuccessful attempt on Hitler's life. And so the weeks went by.

* * *

Mid-June: the three of us went out that morning as usual. We were in good spirits. By the time I got to the Grochow fields, the sun was already high on the horizon; the day promised to be clear and warm. I found a broad meadow with tall grass growing around. A wide, unending green expanse stretched before my eyes; I could see no living soul. I felt happiness in such a spot, far from my enemy, far from those who hunted me down to torture and destroy me. I lay down in the tall, overgrown grass and began thinking about events in history that had taken place on these very fields where I now found myself. Polish fighters had shed their blood here in battles against Russian armies.

I lay in the field till late afternoon, and then, well rested, I found my way back to our cellar. The news awaiting my return put a speedy end to my tranquillity.

An atmosphere of grief and melancholy pervaded the janitor's house. He stood in a corner with his two children and my friend Chill's ten-year-old son. Their faces were pale and their eyes full of tears. They told me that during the course of the day, Chill and Mietek, had taken a long walk together and then gone into a park on Genewska Street to rest for a while. Suddenly they found themselves surrounded by German police. Apparently people living in the vicinity of the park have alerted the police about two suspicious looking characters.

Sensing the danger, Chill jumped up and began to run off. Immediately, a policeman's bullet cut him down. He fell dead. Mietek was caught and sent back to Pawiak where he underwent hellish torture. Several days later he met his death by hanging, just as had the boiler room workers seven months earlier.

The following few lines are devoted to the cherished memory of my two friends: Mietek: childlike, mischievous and always cheerful, yet serious and courageous at fateful moments; Chill: our encyclopedia of knowledge, a brilliant lawyer, true and steady friend, a loving father, doomed to enjoy only the briefest of reunions with his beloved son.

They were the only two casualties of our group of ten escapees. The remaining eight were fortunate enough to hear the ringing of the victory bell one Spring day in May 1945. To all those tortured and persecuted throughout the world, the bell heralded a return to life and liberty.

The death of my two friends was an especially hard blow for me. Not only was I left on my own, but I was forced to abandon our hideout.

It was far too dangerous to spend even one more night there. Quickly I mapped out a course of action. Tonight I would sleep in the same devastated area where we had gone after the Polish police had caught us. I waited until dark and then sneaked into the ruins.

The next morning I went back to the janitor's house where I shaved and washed. Somewhat refreshed, I went off to visit my erstwhile merchant on Marszalkowska Street. He was very happy to see me so, still not mentioning my Jewish origin, I confided some of my problems to him. He promised to find me work and a place to live outside Warsaw. On the spot he gave me the money he had been holding for me all this time.

From there I proceeded to Mrs. Sobolewska's on Zurawia Street. I found her at home and she, too, was glad to see me. I told her that due to my organizational work I had had to travel about the countryside for a while, but that I would like to rest at her place for a few days. She gave me the few things which she had kept for me: my shaving kit, some underwear, other everyday necessities. The week I spent at Mrs. Sobolewska's greatly exhilarated me, both physically and spiritually. At long last I could experience once again the taste of a normal human existence. I slept in a clean bed, and was able to wash myself thoroughly and shave every day. At the end of a week, I decided to return to Saska Kepa. I thought that if they had not looked for me there up to now, everything would be forgotten and I could start afresh.

I left Mrs. Sobolewska's flat with a small package under my arm. First of all, I wanted to go to Powisle, to have a look at my brother's old flat. The building on Ludna Street where my brother had his rented room stood open and empty. The walls and ceilings were being plastered; I realized that I would get no information from the workmen. One of the rooms in that apartment, I now remembered, had served as a doctor's office.

I went down to see the janitor. He was the exact counterpart of my Baptist super on Berezynska Street. A well-groomed individual with a finely trimmed mustache, he appeared more like a rich man than a janitor. I didn't dare question him directly about my brother for fear of placing myself in jeopardy. Instead, I pretended to be a patient and asked the janitor for the doctor's new address. The janitor gave me a strange look. "There wasn't a soul left up there," he explained, "because Mr. Koszarski's wife looked like a Jewess."

Koszarski was my brother's "Aryan" name. I understood the courtly janitor's words only too well. I could not free myself of the suspicion that he himself had had a part in my brother's death. I left the place in a hurry. I went back there just one more time, but that was after the liberation of Warsaw. By then the house on 2 Ludna Street was a burned-out shell. I didn't find a living soul there.

It was already July 1944. After my talk with the janitor of 2 Ludna Street, I made my way to Saska Kepa. In the vicinity of the Poniatowski Bridge I stumbled onto some unusual activity. A column of peasant wagoners, their vehicles hitched to weary little horses barely able to drag their loads, streamed toward me. Inside, I could make out the figures of German soldiers, in an unusual state of dishevelment. There were the wounded with bandaged heads, hands and feet — a band of exhausted men, their torn and filthy rags a far cry from the immaculate uniforms of Hitler's heroic Wehrmacht. The condition of the mud-soaked foot soldiers dragging themselves behind the wagons was not much better. With their heavy growth of beard and their burned out eyes, they looked like what they were: the remnants of a defeated army. The Poles gazed at this picture of destruction. They conversed silently among themselves and winked, "The Russians have already entered Lublin."

I entered my Baptist janitor's place in an exalted mood and told him everything I'd just seen. He had a surprise of his own: The woman caring for Chill's son was willing to take me into her house, too. At present she and Lotek were the only ones in the house. Her husband, formerly a high officer in the Polish army, had joined the Polish forces in London.

I moved into my new home that very day. My landlady had set aside a room for me on the upper story of the house. I tried to stay indoors, not give the neighbors a chance to see me. My landlady insisted that I register with the housing authorities. I had the necessary identification card, but it was false. Nevertheless, through some new connection, I was able to file for an application. Half of July had gone before my "protector" registered me. A week later I received a request from the Housing Authority to come to their offices on August fifth. They had probably detected something amiss with my papers.

In a panic, I ran to my protector and asked him for advice. He promised to investigate the matter. Under no circumstances was I to go to the Housing Authority. It now became clear to me that on August fifth I'd have to leave my present residence. I began to look around for a new place. I had no success, so I thought I'd go back to Mrs. Sobolewska's or stay in my Baptist's cellar for a few days.

The outbreak of the Polish uprising in Warsaw on August 1 was most timely! The German administration of Warsaw had ceased to exist; its offices were all closed. Communication links with the rest of Poland were cut off; the Housing Authority no longer posed a problem.

The Polish Underground Army never succeeded in

kindling the flame of rebellion in the neighborhoods of the right bank of the Vistula. On Saska Kepa it was quiet. All we heard were explosions and the whine of artillery coming from the other side of the river.

On the third or fourth day of the uprising, thick smoke began to envelop various parts of Warsaw. From the terrace of my room I had a good view of the other side of the river: I could see the black columns of smoke rising until the sky was covered with them.

At night the whole landscape was bathed in the red light of the flames that enveloped Warsaw. Then, in the middle of August, Russian planes began to appear overhead. At first they fired only flares, which lit up the area very brightly. I used to sit on my terrace all night and observe the great bonfire.

The Germans left us alone throughout most of August. We had hoped that they would not harass the civilian population here but it was not long before they began to remember us. Toward the end of August, when the nights and early mornings were cool, they began taking away all the men up to fifty years of age. One morning a German soldier showed up on our street and ordered us to assemble on Francuska Street. My first reaction was not to go. I began looking for a hiding place. I noticed that all the men were preparing to obey the call; by not going to the assembly point, I surely would have drawn unfavorable attention to myself. So I went along.

German soldiers took us to a camp site for Soviet prisoners of war, somewhere in a suburb of Praga. The Soviet prisoners were gone now, but the barracks were full of lice, roaches and other vermin. We made up our beds outdoors and lived that way for a number of days.

I knew that I could not allow myself to be taken away in a transport. Having survived up to now I could not let myself be dragged off once more to a concentration camp. I soon found a good hiding place in the vast camp area. Every morning before roll call I used to crawl into it. After roll call they took the Polish men away with the transport and the soldiers brought in fresh victims. Only then did I dare leave my hole. One day, shortly before the Russian Army's entry into Praga, I succeeded in running away from that camp, too. I did not go back to my previous hideouts. Along with other refugees, I ensconced myself in a house on the edge of the Grochow fields.

One late afternoon in the middle of September 1944, I climbed into the attic. From there I looked down on a broad terrain covered with the lush green of vegetable gardens. Down the street, I saw two German noncoms in shiny boots, pushing a small cannon on two wheels. They were in a great hurry, headed for the direction of the Poniatowski Bridge. I don't know whether they made it across, because in a little while I heard the bridge exploding.

I surveyed the field carefully. At a distance of several hundred meters I noticed that the foliage seemed to be moving northward. "What could that be?" I asked myself. As the "moving grove" advanced, I realized that what I was looking at was actually an army of people inching their way forward, under cover of the green branches. I had just seen the first Soviet patrol.

By next morning, all the streets of Saska Kepa were full of Polish and Soviet soldiers. On that morning I was reborn a free man. I went into the street and joined the great procession of armored cars and heavy artillery. I listened with half an ear only to the talk of the Russian officers praising the heroism of their army. What I wanted was to experience the exaltation of being free. I was free again! so I kept repeating to myself. But still I felt no joy.

As I began to draw up the balance sheet of my life

under the Nazi occupation, it became clear that I had paid too high a price for the freedom I had regained. All my dear ones, without exception, had been annihilated. Could I ever make peace with those tragic facts? Moreover, a second question remained, "Why was it my fate to remain behind as the last representative of my extensive family, the only mourner for our former home?"

I was overwhelmed with doubts and misgivings. I wondered whether it was worthwhile carrying on the superhuman struggle, to hold on to life. Would mankind ever appreciate and understand the value of our sacrifice?

Julien Hirshaut
Summer 1944
after escape from Pawiak

Part IV

APPENDIX

Chapter 23

Documents Relating To Pawiak

Documentation for the Pawiak prison chronicle is very limited. The Warsaw Gestapo archives were burned by the Nazis themselves during the evacuation, and the archives of the prison administration office lie somewhere under the rubble of the jail blown up by the Nazis prior to their departure from Warsaw. Only the archive of the "Prison Unit of the Polish Underground Government" were found after the war. That archive consists chiefly of "Reports from Pawiak," which were put together from the *gryps* smuggled out of the prison.

Jews were not the only victims of Pawiak; this prison served as the chief torture center for Poles in the capital city. During the five years of the occupation, the very best of the Polish intelligentsia, political leaders, fighters for the liberation of Poland, passed through Pawiak on their way to German concentration camps. For many of them Pawiak was their last stop before being killed.

After the war there appeared in Poland hundreds of newspaper articles and treatises dealing with Pawiak. Most of them are in the form of memoirs kept by Polish prisoners; these memoirs have a certain documentary character and value. Other books exist too, but in all of these publications the role of the Jews is omitted almost entirely, or is just mentioned in passing.

In sum, almost all the informational material related to Pawiak relies on testimony gathered by the Polish Governmental Commission investigating Nazi crimes and, partly, on the Jewish Historical Institute. There exists, however, another private file of documents regarding Pawiak. This file was created by Bronislav Anlen, Jewish dentist from Warsaw and former prisoner. Anlen was imprisoned in Pawiak in November 1943 and remained in Block Eight until the prison was blown up. Anlen (known as "Bronek") and his closest friend Leon Guttman ("Lutek") deserve special recognition and grateful remembrance in this chronicle.

Leon Guttman was appointed clerk of cell Blocks Seven and Eight in the spring of 1944. The Germans, for reasons of their own, thought it advisable to retain Jews in certain jobs. Appointing as clerk a Jewish prisoner, they reasoned, would be a good way to prevent the Polish prisoners from having contact with each other. A Jew, a man under threat of death, would not risk his life to help a Polish prisoner whose stay in Block Seven was, in any case, limited to the two weeks needed for the investigation of his crimes.

But here the Germans miscalculated. Not only did Lutek do nothing to prevent such contacts, but he took an active part in arranging them. According to Leon Wanat, chief clerk of the prison administrative office, Leon Guttman was one of the chief pillars of all the conspiratorial activities in Pawiak. Bronek Anlen and Lutek were the orderlies of Block Seven and Eight. Anlen too lent a hand in the conspiratorial work; former Polish prisoners remember him with gratitude even today for the invaluable help he gave them.*

At the end of July 1944 Lutek and Bronek along with the remaining Jewish craftsmen were trans-

* See his book, *Behind Pawiak Walls* (Warsaw, 1960).

ferred to the Gesia camp. There they were freed by the Polish rebels and took part in the uprising. Lutek was killed but Anlen survived the war. He assumed the task of researching the Pawiak story; he worked with reverence and dedication, actually seeking out every living soul who could tell him something about the place. He also solicited countless depositions in writing from many people who had since left Poland and were now living in various parts of the world.

If the aforementioned archive of the "Prison Unit of the Polish Underground Government" is at all known today to the public, it is only due to the efforts of Anlen. He found the materials in the archives of the Communist Party, deciphered the code used in the reports of the "Prison Unit," and then rewrote the material in clearer style for inclusion in his archive. The reports take up 571 typewritten pages, of which about thirty-seven were published in two editions of the magazine *Kultura* (fifteenth and twenty-second of August 1965).

Anlen's private file is of greater significance for information on the history of Pawiak during the Nazi occupation than all other public files combined.

Most of the materials making up the separate Pawiak files were reconstructed after the war; only the reports from the "Prison Unit," originate from the time of the occupation. Because of that, their value for historical research purposes is considerably higher than that of the reconstructed materials.

Essentially, the prison "Underground" became an integral link in the Polish Underground Espionage Service, which was working so diligently for an Allied victory. Its chief task was to find out what was happening to the military and political activists imprisoned in Pawiak. The continued existence of Underground positions in Warsaw and throughout Poland, depended on the outcome of the Gestapo investigations.

Witold Bienkowski performed wonders with his in-prison information network. The communications services, also organized by him, enabled prisoners to smuggle their *gryps* out of the prison and, in return, receive messages and instructions sent to them by the Polish Underground. The various individuals who performed these services during the five years of the occupation did so fully conscious of the risks. Many of them were Poles whom the Germans kept on at their pre-war jobs at Pawiak. These people were taken to and from work in special cars and used the opportunity to take the mail in and out of prison.

Before the liquidation of the ghetto, those who "commuted" daily to and from the prison — Jewish craftsmen, doctors and other medical personnel — served as clandestine "mail carriers." Moreover, states Wanat, in his book *Behind Pawiak Walls*, Jews relayed private messages from prisoners to their families, and in return brought the inmates medicines, cigarettes and news of their dear ones. Wanat singles out three Jewish tailors: Szymon Hochman, Szymon Berenstein and Julek Haber among this group of liaison personnel. But these communication channels broke down after the destruction of the ghetto: the medical personnel was then reduced to doctor-prisoners and craftsmen who worked on the premises of the prison. Polish guards or *Klawish* took over the work of maintaining these vital links with the "outside."

Most of the "Report from Pawiak" came from *Serbia* or the women's section. Thanks to the women guards, *Serbia* enjoyed the most successful liaison with the free world. In general, female guards outshone their male counterparts in the fulfillment of their patriotic duties. Many courageous, devoted women gave their lives to the cause of freedom. Reports of political significance, however, always came from the men's section, Wanat's domain. He always had access to documents, notes from the prisoners and the like. He made copies of the more important documents whenever possible and sent them out through existing channels to the underground.

The underground work inside the prison was most successfully concentrated in the two hospitals (one for men and one for women). Both the doctor-administrators and the orderlies enjoyed relative freedom of movement and maintained continuous contact with all the prisoners. They could visit, or send for, any but the most stringently isolated of the prisoners. Moreover, a lively interchange existed between the two hospitals.

Nevertheless, one should not overestimate the value of these prison "Reports" in any investigation of the Pawiak story. Some of the information does not merit complete credibility. "Objective" and "subjective" materials must be evaluated individually. The data based on documents, records and statistics copied from the prison files is generally reliable, except where a name or a statistic was incorrectly transcribed. More caution should be exercised in the evaluation of the descriptive and anecdotal materials. It was inevitable that stories handed down by word of mouth would undergo subtle transformation before reaching the recorder.

Consider, too, the psychological condition in which the prisoners found themselves. Removed from a normal life, shut behind high walls and iron gates, under constant threat of physical torture and death, those prisoners easily lost the ability to make realistic evaluations. As the difference between reality and fantasy became blurred they became increasingly susceptible to accepting as fact some purely imaginary tale.

Let me cite an example. In a "Top Secret Report" from Pawiak dated June 2, 1944, we read, "On Wednesday, May 30th we received the following information from the prison area: 'During the course of the day, ten Jews from the men's section, disguised in Nazi uniforms, escaped, after having cut through the window bars. They were picked up by a car which came right up to the prison gate. One must assume that that little operation was carried off by the Communists.'"

The event just described is very well known to the author of this book — he was one of those who escaped! The getaway is fully described in Chapter 22 of this book (*The Escape*). Anyone who compares the two sources can see that only the bare facts correspond to what really happened that day; the other details are completely the figment of someone's imagination: We didn't escape by day, but by night. We had no Gestapo uniforms, nor did we have any contact with any political organization. So we fled on foot in our bedraggled civilian clothes; no automobile was waiting for us. The truth is that we had no contact with the Communist Party, nor did the Communists help us in any way.

The problems faced by the Jewish prison community are, for the most part, ignored. Only in "extraordinary" cases does the fate of the Jewish prisoner merit more than perfunctory attention. One must remember that the "norm" for Jew and Pole was never the same. The shooting of fifteen to twenty Jews, an event which regularly took place every morning in the ruins of the ghetto, was looked upon as a "normal" occurrence and thus went unrecorded. These executions could evoke no untoward reaction on the part of our chroniclers. An example: the "Report" of August 7, 1943, tells us that "on August 6 Helena Jaguczanska was carried out to her execution on a stretcher and shot, along with the daily quota of Jewish women." In general, there had to be a dramatic rise in the number of Jews being killed before the event was recorded in the "Reports." "On August 4th there was a new execution of a greater number of Jews and people suspected to be of Jewish origin. In a *gryps* that reached us from underground sources in prison, the following is reported: 'together with the Jews a few Poles are now being executed. Their names cannot be identified because they were brought directly from Szuch avenue (Gestapo Headquarters) and are not included in the prison files.'"* Again, the cynical mass murder of the "Hotel Polski" Jews receives no more than perfunctory documentary treatment in the "Reports." The Jews from "Hotel Polski" were brought to Pawiak in the afternoon of July 13, 1943. On July 15th they were shot by the hangman Alberts in the ruins of the house on 27 Dzielna Street.

Researchers do not agree on the total number of Jews exterminated in this affair. My estimates of three hundred Jews killed was based on Anlen's analysis of the "Reports" which state that four hundred Jews were brought from "Hotel Polski" to Pawiak. Ninety-five of them were accepted as citizens of foreign countries and taken to the "Internee Pavilion" in the women's section. The rest, i.e. three hundred five, were shot.

Leon Wanat's figures are somewhat different. According to Wanat, a total of four hundred twenty-four persons were arrested in "Hotel Polski." Two hundred sixty-two had their ID papers voided by Brand and his assistants and were shot two days later.

* These must be Poles accused of helping Jews — J.H.

The remaining one hundred sixty-two were interned as foreign nationals. It is really difficult to gauge the accuracy of these numbers. The answer must lie somewhere in between.

The location of the execution site receives some clarification in the "Reports." Where in the demolished ghetto did the Germans carry out the executions? According to information I received, there were two such places; the ruins of the houses on 25 and 27 Dzielna Street and the former Jewish community house at 19 Zamenhof Street. It may be noted here that the *Befehlstelle* carried out their job of burning the corpses at Zamenhof Street.

The "Reports" mention three additional execution sites — 22 Gesia Street, 3 Dzika Street and 2 Nowolipki Street. I do not think these sites were used frequently. We are also told that the victims of the executions were buried in the Jewish cemetery on Okopowa Street (the Gesia Cemetery). That proposition may be rejected out of hand. In no way can it be reconciled with the German policy of burning the bodies in order to eliminate all traces of their crimes.

One of the most difficult tasks for the researcher into the Jewish annihilation is to establish accurate statistical data. Only in rare instances is it possible to come up with even reasonably accurate figures. In dealing with the "Jewish Question," the Germans were not interested in statistics; the goal was to kill all Jews, exact numbers were irrelevant. Very seldom, therefore, are totals given in German documents relating to Jews. When such figures *are* given, they are neither reliable nor accurate.

If we could establish the number of Jews who were brought to Pawiak in the period following the destruction of the ghetto in May 1943, until the end of the German occupation in July 1944, we would have the answer to two important questions. First, how many Jews were captured in Warsaw on the "Aryan" side (all these Jews were brought to Pawiak). Second, how many Jews died in Pawiak? (All Jews brought in, except for a small number of artisans who were employed in the prison and whose number is known to us, were killed.

I doubt whether we could arrive at the proper figure even had the prison archives been preserved. The Jews in the death cells were not individually listed in the prison files. The Germans sent out only total figures with the qualification "plus." The chief guard who drove the prisoners from Gestapo H.Q. to Pawiak used to receive a list containing the names of the arrestees "plus" a certain number (e.g. "plus twenty" meant that the transport for that day included twenty Jews for the "Aussiedlung").*

In the same way, the Jews were tallied in the daily prison complement: so many arrestees "plus twenty." If no execution took place on a given day, the same Jews remained the next day. Let us say that the following day another ten Jews arrived. In that case, the tally for that day would show thirty. So that even if we had all the daily reports of the full prison complement in hand and could add up the number of "pluses" for all those days, the sum would still be inaccurate. The number of Jews from the days when no executions took place would be doubled or even tripled, because sometimes executions were arranged for every third day. So it's all the more difficult to determine any figure whatsoever since no documents from the prison administration office were ever recovered.

Judging from my experience in the death cell, my own estimate is that a minimum of five hundred Jews

* Deportation and extermination.

227

a month passed through the Pawiak prison. That would bring the total to seven thousand for the fourteen months in question.

My estimates seem confirmed by the "Reports of the Polish Underground Prison Unit." Let us accept as a certainty that the number of Poles who were executed never exceeded the number of Jews killed.* The following figures appear in a "Report": 5,672 men and 287 women killed, a total of 5,959. The "Report" states that no Jews are included in these figures.

Today we are not in a position to establish accurate numbers for the Jewish work groups at the end of Pawiak's existence. When I escaped from Pawiak with the ten men on May 30, 1944, another one hundred eighty-two men and women remained in the Jewish work group in prison. Of that number, forty-two men were shot on July 14th.

On July 30th, sixteen men, led by the shoemaker Gutman, fled through the excavated tunnel into the city canals. So a group of one hundred twenty-four men and women remained in Pawiak. On July 31, 1944 they were evacuated to the Gesia concentration camp and on August 5, 1944, they were freed by the Polish rebels. The attack on the Gesia camp was carried out by the "Zoska" battalion with the help of two tanks from the Panzer Division under the command of Lt. Wacek.**

* An exception may be made for the period following the Polish uprising in Warsaw on August first 1944.
** See: Bronislav Anlen "On the Twentieth Anniversary of the Pawiak Action," Wojskowy Przeglad Historyczny, No. 4, Warsaw 1964, (a military historical publication).

Chapter 24

Uprising in Block Three

The uprising in Block Three took place twelve days before the outbreak of the Polish rebellion in Warsaw. [August 1, 1944]. I was no longer in Pawiak prison at the time, so I cannot give a firsthand account. Right after the liberation, however, I met with several old friends who were present during these momentous events.

From these friends I received reports, somewhat contradictory in nature it must be admitted, about the revolt. Not until the end of the fifties and the beginning of the sixties did* Bronislaw Anlen investigate the matter more closely.

The following account derives from a comparison of the portions of the Anlen Archive and the reports of my friends.

Plans to organize a military attack on the prison had been under consideration by the Polish Underground Army throughout the five years of the German occupation; they were never carried out. Nor did the uprising in Block Three contribute much to their realization, as will be seen in the account that follows.

On the crucial night, the Pawiak prisoners were awakened by the sound of gun fire and grenades exploding. There was no doubt that a major battle was taking place. The prisoners of the Polish Underground were about to wage a battle for thir liberation.

* Anlen's research is discussed in more detail in chapter 23.

Soon, it seemed, all the prisoners would be set free.

Several hours passed in this way. The shooting increased in intensity, then gradually subsided. The cells in the prison blocks remained closed; nobody came to lead the prisoners out of jail.

The next morning an extraordinary situation prevailed throughout the prison. No one offered any explanations for the events of the previous night. There was just talk of a rebellion in Block Three (the block in which were sequestered the soldiers and officers of the Underground Polish Army). The leaders of the uprising were the prison clerk Marian Frank from Block Three and the Ukrainian guard, Ivan Petrenko. The rebels, apparently, had been armed. Rumor had it that the uprising had been organized with the sanction of the A.K. (Polish Underground Army).

But the promised help from outside never arrived; the rebels of Block Three fought alone, and lost. I quote verbatim from the July 25, 1944 "Report"* issued by the "Prison Unit of the Polish Underground Government."

"On the night of July 19th and continuing into the 20th, an unsuccessful attempt at a revolt took place from the inside. It proceeded as follows:

"About 1:20 A.M. Ivan Petrenko, the Ukrainian chief guard who stood watch in Block Three, opened the door to one of the cells and released two of its prisoners, a Pole and a Jew. The Ukrainian corridor guards refused to release the three men from the block, he was killed instantly. The shooting alerted Gestapo personnel, among them an SS officer who happened to be present. They came running within seconds and opened fire inside Block Three. Tens of people were killed and wounded. The Germans lost

* Six days before the Warsaw Uprising.

several men, among them the aforementioned SS officer. All participants in the revolt were killed.

"At the same time the watchtower guards opened fire; they were assisted by a German police squad who had been summoned from town. The shooting lasted till four o'clock in the morning. At the same time, sporadic gunfire could be heard in the vicinity of the ghetto. Automobiles were observed quite close to the aforementioned points.

"After the revolt the Germans carried out personal interrogation in a particularly ruthless fashion in Block Three and throughout the whole prison. The prisoners were led naked into the corridors and held there till the end of the search. Men and women were treated alike. On the morning of July 20th, immediately following these incidents, eighty men from Block Three were taken to the ghetto and shot; in addition eleven women were executed. That same day saw the preparation of a transport of fifty women.* Panic and dejection reigned in the prison. A continuous investigation went on; even those with prison 'jobs' were not permitted to go to work. The sick stayed without medical attention.

"July 21: A Gestapo officer examined the prisoners of Block Three and selected about one hundred eighty men to be shot immediately. The execution took place in the ghetto, between ten and eleven o'clock A.M. The unusual nature of this event may be deduced from the fact that it was carried out by a group of Gestapo prison guards, aided in their task by gendarmes. Fruewirt himself led each of the four groups to the execution. Evidently he took an active roll in the shootings." (End of the cited report.)

Except for certain minor inaccuracies, the above account is substantially correct.

On July 27 1944, the *"Information Bulletin"* (under-

---

* To be sent to concentration camps, J.H.

ground organ of the Commander-in-Chief of the A.K.) carried the following announcement: "On the night of July 20, German and Ukrainian guards provoked an incident which had all the earmarks of a German attempt to foil an attack by the A.K. to liberate some of the prisoners (in Pawiak). Some ten of the prisoners were shot while attempting flight. The A.K. squad suffered certain casualties as well."

The intent of this article was to confuse the public and hide from it the true facts and motivations behind an incident that had become a source of embarrassment and shame to the Army leaders.

The facts now in our possession indicate that the role of the A.K. in the aborted revolt was far more complex and devious. A coup to liberate the Pawiak prisoners had been under consideration by the Army's top leadership since the autumn of 1943. In July 1944, the High Command charged the *Kediv* (Diversion Brigade) with the task: four *Kediv* squads were to come to the assistance of the prisoners in Block Three (led by Marian Frank* and Ivan Petrenko). Captain "Jan," commander-in-charge of *Action Pawiak* planned the assault to coincide with the prison insurrection.

All preparations took place in the greatest secrecy. The four diversion squads held intensive training sessions for the future combatants. Frank's wife played an important role in the whole affair. Thanks to her, contact was established between Petrenko and the A.K. Unfortunately, her intimate knowledge of the interior layout of the prison was never put to the test.

We have today the testimony of a great number of the A.K.'s soldiers who had some connection with *Operation Pawiak*. From it we can reconstruct the events that led to the failure of the revolt.

* M. Frank: Polish lawyer and officer-in-reserve in the pre-war Polish army.

A meeting of all the fighters from the support groups took place on July 19 between ten and eleven. A.M. Petrenko was at the meeting (it was his day off) and picked up a machine gun and a few grenades. Keeping the weapons well concealed he proceeded to Gestapo H.Q. — the cars that brought the guards to and from Pawiak were already waiting. By twelve noon, Petrenko had already assumed his post in Block Three. No change of orders from the underground could possibly reach him anymore.

But, as we know, there *was* a change of orders. About noon, Captain "Jan," met with Colonel "Radoslav," head of the Diversion Brigade. "Radoslav" informed "Jan" that Operation Pawiak had been scrubbed and that all combat units designated for it must be withdrawn. At that late hour it was absolutely impossible to transmit that information to the Pawiak prisoners.

A meeting of all the fighters comprising the task force took place about 5 P.M. Several high officers of the Underground also came to that meeting and confirmed the order to cancel the action. The combat personnel dispersed. But the order to cancel never reached the support groups, who had met for the last time that morning (just as it did not reach the prisoners in Block Three).

What did finally happen? Support group "Osmian" took up its position at the "Powonzki [the non-Jewish cemetery] from which point they were supposed to launch the attack. They found themselves trapped by German fire just as they began unloading their weapons. Some of them were killed; others succeeded in escaping. A few of the wounded were caught and brought to the Pawiak hosptial.

The Pawiak prisoners from Block Three performed their duty honorably. When the time came, they went forth to fight.

*   *   *

Now we shall take up the matter of the supposed German-Ukrainian "provocation." The July 27, 1944 article which appeared in the *"Information Bulletin"* was merely the first of many such attempts to mislead the public. After the liberation, Drs. Sliwicki and Lot issued a similar statement accusing the Germans and Ukrainians of concocting a plot.

The Polish daily *"Gazeta Ludowa"* (People's Paper) of November 4, 1946 carried a letter to the editor in which Dr. Lot stated that the July 19, 1944 revolt was a German plot whose aim was "terrorizing and demeaning the prisoners with a view to foiling their plans." At that time Dr. Lot based his assumption on several pieces of evidence. But his chief proof was the suspicious character of Marian Frank, the leader of the revolt. According to Dr. Lot, no one trusted Frank. The mere fact, wrote Dr. Lot, "that he, a Jew, was appointed clerk of Block Three and served in that function for a number of months caused much talk. For that reason none of the prisoners who had taken part in the conspiratorial movement trusted him. Everyone made an effort to keep him at a distance and warned others about the risk. Ultimate proof of his role in the revolt became obvious during the shooting in Block Three — he, alone of all the leaders, kept himself separate from the rest, even locking himself up in a different cell. Furthermore, he did not commit suicide. On the contrary, he handed himself over to the Germans. He was not shot along with the other prisoners. The following day, before being taken away, he was made to walk in front of the prisoners assembled in the yard. He pointed out more than ten people from Block Three who must have been involved in organizing the revolt. Right after that he was driven away from Pawiak in a separate car. Seemingly he was being taken to Gestapo H.Q. for further questioning.)

As is evident from the article cited above, Dr. Lot had a ready-made indictment against Frank. His accusations were based on the fact that Frank was a Jew and yet a functionary in a completely Polish unit.

Of all the prisoners who were held captive in the Block Three during that fateful night, only three were saved. Two of them were the doctors already mentioned: Sliwicki and Lot; the identity of the third person has never been revealed.

Despite their status as prisoners the two physicians, Drs. Zygmunt Sliwicki and Felician Lot, actually managed the whole medical assistance program in Pawiak. During the day they worked in the prison hospital, which also housed the clinic. At night they returned to their cell in Block Three. During the revolt, the doctors remained locked up in their cell. They could hear the shooting and the explosions that took place quite close to them, but they could not see anything. Only after all the tumult died down did the guards come for the two men. Still in their night clothes, they were ordered to bandage several wounded Ukrainian SS men.

In my capacity as bath attendant I used to meet the two doctors often. I was not aware then that Dr. Lot had been arrested in connection with his activities in a nationalistic radical organization (a rabidly anti-Semitic organization). In all honesty, however, I must admit that during the time I was in Pawiak, I could not point to any discriminatory acts against Jews on the part of those doctors. True, my friend Stanley Osinski, who was there at the same time as I, relates that Dr. Lot threw him out of the hospital on one occasion, when he came to him for help with a cut finger. On the other hand, when one of our friends felt a sudden weakness in the bathhouse, Dr. Lot came to his aid without delay. And when another of our friends in the Jewish group, Nowak by name, developed appendicitis, it was Dr. Lot who operated on him immediately. Generally speaking, performing an operation on a Jew was not permitted. According to Nazi law, a Jew was not even permitted medical help in Pawiak. The doctors had to sneak Nowak in to the operating room in the greatest secrecy; after the operation, his friends carried him back to his cell. Within a few weeks the man had made a complete recovery.

Drs. Sliwicki and Lot were engaged in intensely conspiratorial activities. As you read their memoirs you get the impression that they were convinced that they, and only they, were the truly appointed representatives of the entire Polish Underground in the prison. The truth is otherwise. It was absolutely impossible for such a widely scattered organization as the Polish Underground to rely solely on one contact in the whole of the prison. Consider the most important element in the Polish Underground, the "*Delegation of the London Government-In-Exile*," it alone consisted of many units, each seeking out its own contacts. The two doctors were in fact working for the "Prison Unit of the Delegation."

In those troubled days it was often difficult to know who was working under whose orders; perhaps the doctors themselves did not know. For example, when Marian Frank was seeking help for his planned revolt, he made contact with the underground A.K., itself a unit of the same Underground for which both doctors worked. However, the "Prison Unit" had never been informed about the plans of the Diversion Brigade.

The doctors were unaware of the multitude of allegiances and resulting breakdown in communication. As the underground's official representatives in the prison, surely, they reasoned, *they* would have been informed about an imminent attack on the prison. And perhaps they should have been consulted on so important an undertaking. To them, the revolt smacked of a plot precisely because they were not informed of, consulted about, or included in, its planning and execution.

Why would the Germans have needed it? In order, as Dr. Lot holds, "to terrorize and demean" the Pawiak prisoners? That theory seems preposterous, totally illogical. The Germans had unlimited power to do with the prisoners as they pleased. They used that power very extensively, shooting and slaughtering whomever they wanted. They needed no excuses to justify their deeds. And certainly they didn't need a plot that cost them the lives of several of their men, among them an SS officer.

The accusations against Frank are just as flimsy. Since the second half of 1943, Jewish prisoners had been placed in many jobs in Pawiak, and the fact that Frank was appointed as clerk of Block Three is no indication of his treachery. Dr. Lot himself finally realized that his accusation had no solid foundation. In an interview published in the Warsaw literary journal "Kultura," of March 27, 1966 he admitted that he had no proofs to bolster his theory. Neither he nor any of his close friends ever saw Frank point a finger at anyone. Quite simply, people were talking . . . there were also rumors that Frank had remained alive while all the participants in the revolt died. That cannot be substantiated either: no one ever saw Frank after the outbreak of the revolt in Block Three.

I hope the present memoir will contribute to the rehabilitation of such valiant fighters as Marian Frank and Ivan Petrenko. They have earned the right to a far more honored place in history than Dr. Lot and his friends would have us believe.

And yet several questions remain unanswered. In the first place, is Frank to be considered a Jew? He had converted to Christianity many years before I met him in Pawiak. Henry Finkelstein, a fellow prisoner, filled in many of the blanks in Frank's biography: never in his life did Frank have any relationship with Jews or Judaism. He had a law degree but never practiced his profession; before the war he had occupied a high position in the Polish Foreign Ministry. In pre-Hitler years Polish society looked upon Frank as one of its own, a "full-fledged Pole." Such situations took an entirely different turn in the era when Hitler's doctrine was operative. The "stigma" of Judaism was carried even by third-generation Christians. It has been said that although Hitler conquered and occupied Poland, he did not subdue the Polish people. That is not entirely correct. Hitler's race theory found very favorable ground in Poland. Perhaps Dr. Lot was not aware of how much he had been influenced by Nazi race theory.

It must be mentioned here that the majority of the Jews, who were imprisoned and died in Pawiak, were there only because they were denounced to the Nazis by Poles. The German occupiers had difficulty in distinguishing between Jew and non-Jew.

* * *

In conclusion, what was the real reason for calling off the attack on Pawiak prison? According to the findings of Bronislaw Anlen, the underground leadership issued the order to storm the prison only half-heartedly; they had little confidence in the success of the mission they were sponsoring. As Colonel "Radoslav" declared in 1962, such an attack would have required the deployment of a great many forces and the availability of heavy arms, none of which the underground possessed in sufficient numbers. From the start, then, preparations for the attack were inadequate. As soon as it became clear that the underground would be involved in a full-fledged uprising to take place on August first, the leadership decided to call off *Operation Pawiak*; it could not afford to diffuse its forces only several days before that momentous event.

The ill-timed cancellation order resulted in the useless loss of life. Had it been issued at the proper time, *all* parties concerned could have reflected before committing themselves to a battle synonymous with suicide. With its "plot" theory, the *"Information Bulletin"* wanted only to deflect the attention of the public from the negligence of the underground leadership. I do not believe that any of the participants in this affair will ever be in a position to exculpate themselves.

Chapter 25

A Travesty of Justice

It is 1972. Almost thirty years have passed since the events described in this book took place. I have been called as a witness for the prosecution in the trial against two of the murderers, Ludwig Hahn and Thomas Wippenbeck. These men have nothing in common but their participation in the atrocities committed against Jews of Warsaw. Both are alive today. Hahn is a wealthy man. Wippenbeck, an underling in the Nazi machine, was and remains a poor man.

Ludwig Hahn, former commandant of the security police (Gestapo) in the city of Warsaw, held the degree of Doctor of Jurisprudence. During the years of his bloody reign in Warsaw, from 1941 to 1944, the security police under his command either slaughtered on the spot, or sent to the death camps of Treblinka and Majdanek, at least three hundred fifty thousand Jews. At least 100,000 Poles, among them thousands of Jews, were incarcerated in Pawiak prison; of these a minimum of forty thousand were shot forthwith and the remaining sixty thousand expedited to concentration camps. The figures cited are minima; their accuracy is not questioned by anyone.

As commandant of the Gestapo, Hahn was directly responsible for all those murders. Moreover, his subordinates share his guilt; they committed their crimes willingly, under orders of their chief.

Thomas Wippenbeck had the necessary prerequisite for the position of prison guard — innate sadism. He received special training in the "art" of torture through courses given to SS personnel and Nazi concentration camp guards.

In addition to the perverted acts mentioned in chapter 17, Wippenbeck personally participated in executions of Poles and Jews — he shot and hanged people. Those Pawiak prisoners who survived the disaster are living testimony to the crimes he perpetrated.

I prepared for my trip to Hamburg in a somber, pessimistic mood. I had no illusions about the conduct or the outcome of these trials. I knew that there was only lukewarm interest for them in the Germany of the seventies.

Statistics published in German newspapers and magazines indicated that of the total of two thousand Nazi criminals against whom any kind of trial proceedings were launched, no more than twenty-one were tried between 1966 and 1972; of those only nine were sentenced (according to figures cited in the magazine *Der Stern*).

When I arrived in Hamburg, it became clear to me that my misgivings were justified; a travesty of justice was in the making.

* * *

Originally indicted on charges of having committed the most heinous crimes, Hahn and Wippenbeck had managed to live openly as free men in the twenty-seven years following the war. One could almost say they had reached the Biblical "full measure of years."

They say that Hahn is a rich man. It is no surprise to me. The property stolen from the Jews of Warsaw couldn't have disappeared from the face of the earth. Where was it kept hidden? If not in its entirety, a part had to be in someone's possession, and who more likely than the chief thug? Today Hahn has his own insurance agency in Hamburg and a villa in the suburbs. His wealth is registered in his wife's name; officially, he is a poor man. The fees for his defense lawyers must have been paid by the government. This was not a modest fee, either — the chief defense attorney received four hundred marks (a good sum for the time) for every day spent in court.

If the German government wants to conduct such a show trial, Hahn must have thought to himself, let it pay. And pay it did. It is said that the trial costs, up until the time of my testimony, had exceeded a million marks. How much more would it cost before the end? Was the life of two murderers worth such an expense?

Wippenbeck, the second accused, is not rich; his threadbare clothes and sunken cheeks testify to it. Before 1939, he worked in a linoleum factory somewhere in Bavaria, a job he resumed after the war as though nothing had happened. Life went on, he completed forty-two years of service and happily became a pensioner. Wippenbeck claims that anyone making inquiries at the factory about his character would not hear a single unkind word.

* * *

German Justice was in no rush to conduct trials against Nazi war criminals. The proceedings against Hahn and Wippenbeck had been in progress since 1959. In that year the Hamburg prosecutor took over the investigation. About one hundred thirty volumes of records accumulated during those years. The accused were placed under investigative arrest on two separate occasions, in 1960-61 and then in 1965-67. Finally, they went free, having paid a paltry sum for bail. The court of appeals issued the writ of release on the ground that the prosecution was taking too much time in preparation for the trial.

At the time of the first investigative arrest certain

bizarre occurrences took place which aroused comment in the liberal German press. While Hahn was in jail, his insurance business had been conducted by a friend, a high-ranking judge in the Hamburg real estate court. A notable of the criminal court "mistakenly" sent Hahn a package of records containing detailed testimony of great importance. The package then was found, at a later investigation, in Hahn's villa, but was left in his possession.

By now it becomes understandable why preparation for the trial lasted a full thirteen years. In fact, without the intervention of Simon Wiesenthal, head of the Center for Documentation in Vienna, the trial might never have gotten under way. In January 1971, when the West German Chancellor Willie Brandt was preparing for his trip to Poland, Wiesenthal wrote to ask him his intentions with respect to the Hahn trial. Only after that letter was made public, did the trial begin assuming a semblance of reality.

Things were not entirely bleak, however. When I registered at the hotel where a room had been reserved for me, I was handed a letter that had been awaiting my arrival. The letter was written in German. Its contents, translated into English, are as follows:

> Esteemed witness! After many years you have come to our country to help us throw light on a small fraction of the crimes committed during the last war. The fact that you voluntarily undertook this difficult journey into a past we all share makes you a very welcome guest in our midst. I am the spokesman for a number of citizens of Hamburg who wish to offer you their services immediately. They intend to be present at the trial proceedings.
>
> We can help you in several ways:
>
> 1. by placing at your disposal a chauffeured automobile.

2. by depositing money in a bank for your expenses.
3. by providing medical services and any needed medication.
4. by taking you on a tour of Hamburg.
5. by giving any necessary advice.

With most cordial greetings,
Giesela Wiese

The letter succeeded in improving my emotional frame of mind. Although I foresaw no immediate need for any of the services offered, I immediately called the writer of the letter. We arranged to meet.

Two young women turned up at the hotel: Mrs. Wiese, the signatory to the letter and Miss Marlene Engel. They told me that they constituted the nucleus of a group of fifteen or so concerned young people in Hamburg. By acquiring a deeper understanding of the Nazi program of Genocide, particularly as it was applied to the Jews, they hope to "raise the consciousness" of the German population. They want to publicize these trials, to have as many people present as possible. Perhaps in response to her campaign, an entire class, accompanied by their teacher, was present while I was on the stand. I am told my testimony made a strong impression on that audience.

And yet, Mrs. Wiese was not too optimistic about the success of her program in general.

Although the neo-Nazi movement had not struck deep roots among the German youth, on the whole they have remained indifferent to her ideals, Mrs. Wiese explained. West Germany was enjoying great prosperity; the chief concern of the younger generation was achieving a comfortable, even affluent lifestyle. The controversies Mrs. Wiese was experiencing with the local newspapers reflects the detachment of present day German society from its Nazi past.

A press representative attended the first day of the proceedings of the current Hahn-Wippenbeck trial; an article appeared in the *Hanse-Stadt Hamburg* paper wherein mention was made of the testimony given by Leon Tishko, former secretary to Adam Cherniakow (chairman of the Warsaw "Judenrat"). Incidentally, Tishko was the first Jewish witness put on the stand. But that was the first and only time that a newspaper reporter showed up in the courtroom; no further accounts of the trial appeared.

So, Mrs. Wiese began to protest. She approached the editors of all the papers, asking, demanding, appealing. Her arguments, however, fell on deaf ears; she received the same answer from everyone, "We have to print what the public wants to read."

The morning after my arrival in Hamburg was my day in court. After two hours of answering questions put to me by the presiding judge, Dr. Flambeck, I was back in the past, my whole mind and all my being immersed in experiences which belong to the past, but continue to live inside me. Recessed in a corner of my soul, they call to me, torturing and haunting me. Now I began truly to appreciate the help brought me by Mrs. Wiese's group of young people. They stood by me, but did not ask any questions.

When I had concluded my testimony, one of the young escorts said, "It's quite remarkable; the witness' statements leave no impression on the accused. It is the witnesses themselves who leave the courtroom depressed and sick."

I had no opportunity to look at myself in the mirror, but I must have looked pretty awful for such a thought to occur to anyone. I made no comment, but I thought to myself, "Why not? The accused have no feelings of remorse and their consciences don't hurt them. Their only regret is that they did not manage to finish us all off — the surviving remnant is present, stalking through the courtroom today. And we, the so-called witnesses? We are tortured not only by having to relive those terrible years, but by feelings of undefined guilt. Every one of us has lost some or all of his near ones; we ask ourselves the same questions over and over: why they, and not I? Have I done all I could to save them?"

And now, in this courtroom, these incompletely healed wounds are reopening. Despite the judges' apparent courtesy and attempts to put me at ease, I collapsed into a state of nervous exhaustion at the conclusion of each interrogation. My hands began to tremble and I had to ask for a short recess. On the other hand, when the defense attorney began lashing out at me with questions designed to catch me in contradictions, I stayed completely calm and defiant.

What of the accused? What is their state of mind? The issues seem foreign to me, practically non-existent. When asked to enter his plea, Hahn proclaims complete innocence. As for Wippenbeck, he heard many witnesses, myself included, testify that they had seen him hang people on the gallows. Faced with definitive proof of his guilt, Wippenbeck steadfastly continues to deny it.

Does behavior such as this partake of arrogant shamelessness? Or is it a form of gallows humor; perhaps it is a combination of both.

After all, wasn't Hahn's entire existence for the past twenty-seven years a display of brazen arrogance? At first, he did not dare use his own name. With the formation of the Republic of West Germany, he came out of hiding; he conducted his insurance business openly, under his own name. He no longer had to fear trial in the courts of an occupying power. What is more, Hahn insisted, he had nothing to fear even from a German court. And until 1960, his instincts proved correct; he emerged unscathed from his encounters with the Law.

German dislike of probing too deeply into the Nazi past certainly contributed to Hahn's peace of mind. Too much "unpleasantness," too many unsavory details were bound to surface during intensive investigations. Some Germans even argue that it is time to forget the past. After all, they say, thirty years have gone by since Hitler's defeat; all those dreadful events took place in wartime — abnormal times breed abnormal behavior. What's more, those Nazis being hunted down, in the interim, have become old and gray. Leave them be.

Such a merciful attitude toward Nazi mass murderers could never bring solace to the victims. And German constitutional law sides with the victim. The crime of murder is excluded from the statute of limitations. It follows, that anyone guilty of mass murder must necessarily bear the responsibility for his crime. In practice, however, German justice goes its own way tempering with mercy the sentence meted out to the killers, the courts absolves them of guilt wherever feasible.

I came to Hamburg from far off New York. I spared no effort in hope that the truth might be revealed. I am a witness for the prosecution.

Who are the three judges, Dr. Flambeck with a perpetual smile on his lips, and his two colleagues, Bartells and Mazolakis? What were they doing while I was in Pawiak?

I answer the questions put to me; I tell the court all I know. I am prepared for heavy cross examination by the defense, but meanwhile, the presiding judge, always with that same smile on his lips, is doing the interrogation. He asks leading questions, seems bent on pushing me into a corner. The events I describe took place thirty years ago. During a previous investigative hearing, held five years earlier, I may have testified that the color of a particular guard's uniform was grey, that it had three stars on the collar; today I describe it as green. Do such minor discrepancies have any bearing on the central issue of the case? Why should I be expected to remember such trivial data? It is a curious reversal: the witness, not the accused, seems to be standing trial. Such questions are quite enough to throw the witness off balance. He begins to act defensively; this attitude in turn, worsens his position. The judge has achieved his objective: to cast doubt on the witness' credibility.

It never occurred to me, while the hearings were in progress, that the judge might be out to "get" me. I assumed rather, that his method of interrogation was normal procedure in a West German court of law.

Once I had an opportunity to read through the entire court proceedings, it became obvious to me that the judge's manner of interrogation differed markedly from witness to witness. Only Jews and Poles were subject to the kind of "cross questioning" I described above. Fortunately, I did not falter and kept composure throughout. At the end of my testimony the chief justice administered an oath, which in the German criminal court system is proof of the witness' credibility. My testimony was not thrown out of court.

Other Jewish witnesses did not fare as well. The aforementioned Dr. Leon Tishko is a good example. With his intimate knowledge of the Warsaw ghetto and the relationship of the "Judenrat" to the Gestapo and to Hahn in particular, Dr. Tishko should have been the star witness in Hahn's trial. He began his testimony with an account of the frightful conditions existing in the Warsaw ghetto: the selections, the deportations, executions. Dr. Flambeck, the presiding judge, interrupted him from time to time with the same insistent question, "Is the witness sure of what he is saying? Does not his memory deceive him on occasion?" Not so, he remembered everything perfectly well, Dr. Tishko declared and continued in this way for a while. Suddenly, the judge reached for a file and extracted from it a sheet of paper which he then flashed in front of the witness.

"I have here witness Tishko's application for repa-ration payments. He bases his claim on the deterioration of his health and impairment of his memory. Is that correct?" asked the judge. Witness Tishko had nothing further to say. He had disqualified himself.

Despite the fact that, nominally, I had done well in my testimony, I, too, felt defeated. Not I alone, but all of the former prisoners in Pawiak who had come to the trial to testify against the two defendants, Wippenbeck and Hahn.

Against, Wippenbeck, nicknamed "Veshatel"* (hangman) the former prisoners had brought a substantial number of accusations. I was a witness to the hanging of three fellow prisoners.

From the onset the denouement of Wippenbeck's trial seemed predetermined. The court pulled off a procedural ploy by making two trials out of one. Trial number one dealt only with crimes related to Pawiak prison and the Polish rebellion. Instead of dealing with crimes against Jews in general, it took up only the question of the so-called "Hotel Polski Jews," most of whom were killed by Alberts in Pawiak.

All other Jewish matters stemming from Pawiak, including Wippenbeck's murder of the three prisoners, were transferred to trial number 2. Some crucial testimony now inadmissable in the first trial, was thrown out of the second trial as well since Wippenbeck no longer appeared there as an accused: the only

* Pronounced: *véshatel.*

accused at trial number two was Hahn. At the end of trial number one Prosecutor Rolf, stating that he could not furnish proof of Wippenbeck's guilt, dropped the case. And one of the most vicious Nazi murderers went free.

And what of Ludwig Hahn? He was sentenced to twelve years in prison, on one count only: his "collaboration" in the murder of people. He was cleared of all other charges, particularly those involving the actual commission of murder.

The verdict aroused strong protests not only abroad but inside Germany itself. The liberal press was particularly vehement in criticism of the decision. Government circles must have become involved as well. Anyhow, Hahn was tried a second time. For his part in the mass murder of Warsaw Jews he received the much harsher sentence of life imprisonment.

* * *

In general, the court did not believe the Polish or the Jewish witnesses. The judge seemed inclined to accept only those of their remarks which could be interpreted as favorable to the defendant. Conversely, the judge accorded full credence to the testimony of Gestapo and SS personnel, although these were the very men under indictment for genocide. Witnesses for the defense told barefaced lies either out of fear of implicating themselves, or from a desire to help their good friend Hahn.

A person like Hahn does not think of himself as a criminal. He has done no wrong. Quite the opposite, he has done only good. Before the Hamburg trial, Hahn described his previous activities as follows: "We were the handmaidens of the Party. We purified it (Hahn is referring to the *Beer Hall Putsch*). We were busy rooting out the enemies of the government." He was only performing his duty to the "Führer and the

Fatherland." He is being punished only because his Führer and his Fatherland lost the war.

Had Hitler won the war, where would Dr. Hahn be today? And where would hundreds of thousands like him be? Sitting on the summit of Mount Olympus with the world at their feet.

But the God of vengeance, the God of those "accursed Jews" reversed our direction, and now here is Dr. Ludwig Hahn sitting on the defendant's bench like a common criminal, murderer and robber.

With this brand of logic, the murderer makes only one important mistake. He forgets the God of Psalms, 96:13, "Before God, for He cometh to judge the earth. He will judge the world with justice and the nations with His faith." That verse also reveals the order by which the world is governed. Crimes against humanity will *not* go unpunished and the criminal *will* be prosecuted until the account is settled.

Ghetto ruins seen from the Pawiak windows.